NIKI JABBOUR'S
VEGGIE GARDEN
REMIX

NIKI JABBOUR'S
VEGGIE GARDEN
REMIX

224 New Plants to Shake Up Your Garden
and Add Variety, Flavor, and Fun

Storey Publishing

The mission of Storey Publishing is to serve our customers by
publishing practical information that encourages
personal independence in harmony with the environment.

Edited by Carleen Madigan
Art direction and book design by Carolyn Eckert
Text production by Jennifer Jepson Smith
Indexed by Nancy D. Wood

Cover photography by © Philip Ficks, front (top row & bottom left half),
    spine, back (top left & top center), inside front, and inside back;
    © James Ingram/Jive Photographic Inc., front (bottom right half) and
    back (author); and Mars Vilaubi, front (title), back (top right)

Interior and additional photography credits on page 225
Leaf graphic pages 2, 5, and 7 by Carolyn Eckert

Storey books are available for special
premium and promotional uses and for
customized editions. For further information, please call 800-793-9396.

Storey Publishing
210 MASS MoCA Way
North Adams, MA 01247
storey.com

Printed in China by R.R. Donnelley
10 9 8 7 6 5 4 3 2 1

LIBRARY OF CONGRESS CATALOGING-IN-
    PUBLICATION DATA
Names: Jabbour, Niki, author.
Title: Niki Jabbour's veggie garden remix /
    by Niki Jabbour.
Other titles: Veggie garden remix
Description: North Adams, MA : Storey
    Publishing, 2018. | Includes index.
Identifiers: LCCN 2017034219 (print)|
    LCCN 2017047879 (ebook)
    | ISBN 9781612126715 (ebook)
    | ISBN 9781612126708 (pbk. : alk. paper)
Subjects: LCSH: Vegetables. | Vegetable
    gardening.
Classification: LCC SB321 (ebook)
    | LCC SB321 .J32 2018 (print)
    | DDC 635—dc23
LC record available at https://lccn.loc
    .gov/2017034219

dedication

To my family, Dany, Alex, and Isabelle, who understand that all I want for my birthday is a truckload of aged manure.

To my mother, Joyce, and my parents-in-law, Kamal and Noha, who started me on this global gardening path.

CONTENTS

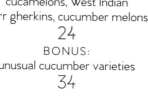

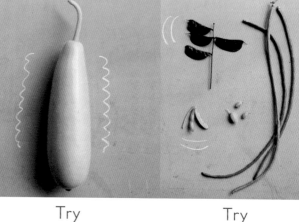

Like cabbage?

Try
Chinese cabbage,
yu choy sum,
komatsuna
138
BONUS: unusual
cabbage varieties
148

Like broccoli?

Try
'Spigariello liscia',
'Piracicaba', Romanesco,
gai lan, sea kale, huauzontle
150

Like potatoes?

Try
Jerusalem artichokes,
groundnuts, Chinese artichokes,
daylily tubers, dahlia tubers
174
BONUS:
unusual potato varieties
184

Like spring radishes?

Try
daikons, black
Spanish radishes
186
BONUS:
unusual radish varieties
193

Like bulb onions?

Try
Japanese bunching onions,
Egyptian walking onions
200
BONUS:
bulb onions
206

Like parsnips?

Try
Hamburg parsley
209

The Snake Gourd That Started It All

It began with a snake gourd — a 5-foot-long vegetable we'd hoped to use as the centerpiece for our Halloween decor. That spring, I'd started the seeds indoors, and by midsummer the rampant vines had reached the top of a sturdy A-frame trellis. Hiding among the large leaves were about a dozen young fruits. It was at this point that my mother-in-law, Noha, dropped by for a garden visit.

Noha grew up in a small village in the mountains of Lebanon, where life revolves around fresh food and family meals, traditions that she continued when she and her husband, Kamal, and their two young sons immigrated to Canada in the 1980s. On this particular day, I had planned to harvest some of the early tomatoes, cucumbers, zucchini, parsley, and salad greens for her. But when she spied the slender gourds, her eyes lit up. She quickly explained that she knew this plant as cucuzza, and in Lebanon, as well as other regions of the Mediterranean, it's grown and eaten like a summer squash. At about a foot in length, the fruits on my vines were just the right size for eating.

Thanks to Noha, I learned that my "ornamental" gourds were also edible, and I was thrilled to share with her a vegetable that she hadn't eaten in decades. I started to think that perhaps there were other Lebanese vegetables I could try in my Nova Scotia garden, and I began researching and asking questions. Soon, I was planting 'Omar's Lebanese' tomatoes, Armenian cucumbers, cousa zucchini, chickpeas, and molokhia — a cooking green Noha uses to make a flavorful chicken stew that is served over rice and topped with toasted pita bread and vinegar-soaked onions.

Branching Out

Like most North American gardeners, my vegetable plots had always been planted with "normal" crops like tomatoes, potatoes, carrots, peas, and beans, and although I played around with different varieties, I certainly didn't venture too far from the traditional veggies. This crash course in global gardening soon had me scheming to branch out and try edibles from other regions like India, Thailand, Mexico, Argentina, Italy, China, and Japan. I requested seed catalogs that specialized in ethnic crops, ordering vegetables and herbs that had maturity dates that I thought would fit in with my climate and gardening zone.

As with most experiments, some things thrived and some things didn't, but my success rates far outstripped the crop failures, and in some cases I was able to prompt long-season vegetables to reach maturity in my short-season garden by using simple season extenders like mini hoop tunnels and row covers. The extra few weeks at the end of the traditional growing season was enough to push crops like chickpeas, Thai eggplants, and certain gourds to reach maturity.

This bounty of international veggies and herbs has allowed me to flex my cooking skills, tackling recipes with ingredients that, in the past, had been difficult to source or expensive to buy. I was surprised how many of these unconventional edibles — pak choi,

mibuna, edamame, bitter gourds, za'atar, yard-long beans, daikon radishes — thrived in my garden, and our backyard soon became known as the experimental farm. Measuring just over 2,000 square feet, the garden isn't huge, but it's enough space to test new-to-me crops as well as grow our traditional family favorites like 'Sungold' tomatoes, 'Napoli' carrots, and 'Purple Podded Pole' beans.

Fast-forward about a decade from that eye-opening day in the garden with Noha, and you'll find Dany and me standing in the garden, thrilled to discover the first Mexican sour gherkin cucumber ready for harvest. Also called cucamelon or mouse melon, these grape-size cucumbers have the mottled appearance of a tiny watermelon.

There was some debate about who should get the first taste, but since marriage is (apparently) about compromise and sharing, we each took a small bite, enjoying the bright burst of cucumber-citrus flavor.

Dany's immediate response was, "Wow! Why don't more people grow these?" Great question! And one that eventually led to this book. Why don't more people grow cucamelons? Or cucuzze? Or herbs for za'atar? Or chickpeas? Or groundnuts? Is it because those are unfamiliar garden crops? Or perhaps gardeners just don't realize the amazing range of food plants that can be cultivated in their gardens? Or maybe because they aren't always readily available in local garden centers?

I always tell gardeners
to visit their local farmers'
market for inspiration.
It's a treasure trove
of potential crops
for your garden.
If your local farmers
can grow it, chances
are you can, too!

4

Diversity in the Vegetable Plot

There is a world of diversity available to gardeners, if we just take the time to look. For example, take the humble pole bean, a common crop across much of North America, the United Kingdom, and Europe. Most of us stick to the standard handful of varieties offered through seed catalogs, but if you just take a moment to look, you'll discover that there is an incredible range of pod colors, shapes, sizes, and flavors just waiting for you.

Have you met 'Gold Marie', a Romano-type bean produced on fast-growing vines? The 1-inch-wide butter-yellow pods have a hearty, meaty texture; with just one bite, this heirloom became a new family favorite. Or 'Red Noodle', a plant with mesmerizing dark red pods that can reach lengths of up to 18 inches? And don't get me started on my obsession with giant lima beans! These 10-foot-tall plants need a long frost-free season, but I still strive (with the help of an early planting in a spring mini hoop tunnel) to grow and harvest this Mediterranean staple. The beans are borne in lengthy, wide pods and, once dried, are a winter favorite. I slowly bake them in a thick tomato sauce

liberally seasoned with fresh basil and aromatic vegetables for a simple, satisfying feast that pairs well with warm, crusty bread.

As I continued to explore the wealth of global crops, I realized that I was making a "Why grow that, when you can grow this?" type of list. Why grow 'Kentucky Wonder' beans, when I can grow 'Jimenez', a unique variety from Spain that bears beautiful green pods boldly brushed in bright red. The broad, flattened beans, which can grow up to an inch wide, are tender and tasty, with a flavor that pairs well with salty pancetta.

Or why grow spinach when I can play with the amazing assortment of greens like amaranth, orach, hablitzia, molokhia, and sweet potato leaves — just to name a few. Unlike spinach, many of these greens are heat tolerant, pumping out fresh foliage all summer long. And some, like hablitizia, are perennial, offering an annual crop of delicious greens.

Or why grow 'Straight 8' cucumbers, a garden standard, when I could grow 'Boothby's Blonde', an heirloom with pale, oval-shaped fruits and a lovely sweet flavor. Or how about Armenian cucumbers, which bear a heavy crop of pale green, heavily ribbed fruits. Botanically a melon, this "cucumber" is the perfect cooling treat on hot summer days. Or why not try growing 'Dragon's Egg' cucumbers for your *Game of Thrones*–obsessed family members and friends. This peculiar variety bears creamy white egg-shape fruits that are mild and bitter-free and, if placed in flames, may hatch into dragons (okay, just kidding about that last part).

Learning from Immigrant Gardeners

Immigrant gardeners generously introduce us to lesser-known crops.

My original interest in growing a wider variety of edibles was sparked by my immigrant in-laws. In home gardens and community gardens across North America and beyond, immigrants bring their rich food traditions to their new countries, growing vegetables and herbs from their homelands. We have much we can learn from these gardeners, who, more often than not, are extremely generous in sharing their expertise and introducing us to lesser-known crops and varieties.

Of course, immigrant gardeners also present us with another learning opportunity: sharing traditional growing techniques. Several methods, such as the African keyhole garden, a plot that combines a raised bed with an active compost system, and hügelkultur, an Eastern European permaculture bed, have become mainstream and are being put to work in gardens from coast to coast.

More recently, I've begun to talk about my experiences with global vegetable gardening at my seminars and workshops. Not sure of the reception I would receive from vegetable gardeners used to more widely known crops and gardening styles, I was initially a bit hesitant. Happily, the response was overwhelmingly positive. I learned that food gardeners are hungry to explore the diversity of vegetables, herbs, and fruits found in our big, wide world. In these pages, I hope that you find the encouragement and inspiration to create your own global vegetable garden.

like tomatoes?

try garden berries!

Ground cherry

Tomatillo

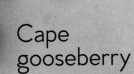

Cape
gooseberry

Not sure when to harvest? It's as simple as gathering up the fallen fruits. Once the fruits have turned from green to gold, they're ready to eat.

L ike me, you may already be experimenting in your tomato patch, trying a mixture of unique heirlooms and hybrid varieties, each of which offers something different and tasty. Tomatoes (along with peppers and eggplants) are one of the most popular crops in the nightshade family, but other members are definitely worth a try! Some tasty ones include the "garden berries": ground cherries, Cape gooseberries, and tomatillos. With all of these plants, keep in mind that although the ripe fruits are edible, all other parts are poisonous.

Glorious Ground Cherry

THE FLAVOR OF a ripe ground cherry is comparable to pineapple with hints of cherry tomato and vanilla. It's an unusual combination, but one that works. Occasionally, I'll bite into an extra-ripe berry that almost tastes like butterscotch — sublime! Their sweet flavor is what earns them the nicknames "strawberry tomato" and "Cossack pineapple." You can eat the fruits fresh or in salads, but you can also turn them into jam, pie, cobbler, or sauce for drizzling over ice cream or cheesecake. If you have a dehydrator, you can dry them and eat them like raisins.

This is a fun and easy crop to grow, with the low, bushy plants producing hundreds of marble-size berries from midsummer until the hard autumn frost. The fruits drop from the plants when they are ripe, hence the name ground cherry. They are firm fruits, even when ripe, with seeds that are so small the fruits actually seem seedless.

TRICKY TO START, BUT SELF-SOWING EVER AFTER

Ground cherries are notoriously tricky to germinate, but a bit of bottom heat will boost germination rates. I sow seeds indoors, 6 to 8 weeks before my last expected spring frost, and help them along by covering the seed trays with clear plastic wrap and placing them on top of my fridge to keep warm. Germination can take 2 to 3 weeks. Once transplanted into the

THE DETAILS

A.K.A.: Husk cherry, *Physalis pruinosa*

DAYS TO MATURITY: 70 days from transplant

HAILS FROM: North America

VARIETIES TO TRY: 'Aunt Molly's', 'Cossack Pineapple'

garden, expect the harvest to begin in 70 to 75 days.

You may need to start them only once, though! Ground cherries are prolific self-seeders, so expect many volunteer plants to pop up the following season. You can either thin them and leave a few in place, or dig them up to share with gardening-minded family and friends. Growing them in containers on a wooden, stone, or concrete deck or patio will minimize the threat of self-seeding.

RELAXED OR TRUSSED UP

The plants have a relaxed growth habit, which can take up a lot of garden space. I use tomato cages (inserted at transplanting time) or insert three 4-foot wooden stakes around the plant and use twine to keep the growth relatively upright. If you do support your ground cherry plants, you can transplant them 2 feet apart. Unsupported plants should be spaced at least 3 feet apart. They don't get very tall (between 1½ and 3 feet in height), and they can also be grown in pots on a sunny deck or patio. Ground cherries pollinate themselves, so small-space gardeners can enjoy this crop, even if they have only one plant.

LOOK DOWN FOR FRUIT

Harvesting is as simple as gathering up the fallen fruits — a favorite activity for our kids! Sometimes the fruits are still immature when they fall and need extra time to ripen from inedible green to rich, golden yellow. You could leave them on the ground for a week or two, but because the squirrels also love this treat, I pick up the fallen fruits every couple of days and bring them indoors to finishing maturing. To keep fallen fruits clean, I apply a straw mulch beneath the plants in early summer. This also helps keep the soil evenly moist, which ground cherries appreciate. To encourage ripe or almost-ripe fruits to fall, you can "tickle" or gently tousle the plant every few days.

If you're not going to eat your whole harvest immediately, store the small fruits, still in husks, in a refrigerator, cool basement, garage, or root cellar. Under ideal conditions, they can store from 6 weeks to 3 months. When frost threatens in autumn, cover the plants with a row cover or frost blanket to protect the crop. This can extend the season for several weeks.

Cape gooseberry

TRY THIS!
Citrusy Cape Gooseberry

IF GROUND CHERRY FRUITS GROW to the size of marbles, Cape gooseberries are closer to that of a cherry tomato. In fact, I find they look very much like 'Sungold' tomatoes when fully ripe; about ¾ inch in diameter, with glossy orange-gold skin. Once ripe, the fruits are more tart than ground cherries, with a flavor that combines the tang of citrus with hints of tomato and pineapple.

Cape gooseberries need a slightly longer growing season than ground cherries; short-season gardeners will find that prewarming the soil before planting will give them a jump on the growing season. To prewarm, lay a piece of black plastic mulch (or even black garbage bags split open) over the bed 2 weeks before you intend to plant. Once the crops are in the ground, a mini hoop tunnel covered in clear plastic can be used to protect plants from the up-and-down temperatures of late spring. Just be sure to open the ends of the tunnel on mild days to allow good air circulation.

GO EASY ON THE NITROGEN . . .

Overall, Cape gooseberry is a low-maintenance crop, needing full sun but growing in a wide range of soil conditions. I dig in a few inches of compost before planting, but no aged manure or high-nitrogen fertilizers. Too much fertilizer will result in lush, vigorous growth but few blossoms. The plants of Cape gooseberry fertilize themselves, but you can boost pollination by giving the plants a gentle shake from time to time.

If garden space is tight, plant them in large pots or planters; they make attractive container plants and can be mixed with other ornamental or edible plants in their pots. Cape gooseberry plants grow more upright than ground cherries do, typically reaching 2 to 3 feet, or even taller in southern regions.

Cape gooseberries can be slow to ripen, especially in northern gardens. If frost threatens while the plants are still heavy with ripening fruit, erect a mini hoop tunnel to shelter the plants. This can be left in place for several weeks as the remaining fruits turn from green to bright gold inside their husks.

Like ground cherries, the fruits are gathered as they fall from the plant. Ripe Cape gooseberries can be stored in a cool site (50°F/10°C) for up to 3 months. They can be eaten fresh, cooked, or dried (toss dried fruits in homemade granola bars or trail mix). Chop fresh Cape gooseberries and add them to leafy or fruit salads, salsa, chutney, or relish. I have a friend who swears that the best way to eat them is to dip the fresh berries into melted chocolate (but isn't everything better dipped in chocolate?). You can also bake them in pies and crumbles or make them into jams and jellies.

THE DETAILS

A.K.A.: Inca berry, Aztec berry, golden berry, *Physalis peruviana*

DAYS TO MATURITY: 70–80 days

HAILS FROM: South America

VARIETIES TO TRY: None

Tangy Tomatillo

AH, TOMATILLO, the starring ingredient in *salsa verde*, the classic Mexican green salsa. By themselves, tomatillos have a tart, citrus flavor, but roast them and pair them with hot peppers, onions, and cilantro, and you've got a dynamite dish that can be added to tacos, served with a bowl of nachos, spooned onto grilled fish or chicken, or used in a thousand other ways to add a bright zip to your cooking.

Straight out of the garden, tomatillos look very much like Cape gooseberries and ground cherries, but they are more the size of golf balls. Another important difference is that the two other species are not eaten while still green, but tomatillos are; if you wait until tomatillos turn pale yellow, they'll be too soft for most dishes and the flavor will have mellowed significantly. You'll also notice that tomatillo fruits fill out their husks as they grow, often splitting the papery wrapper as they approach peak ripeness. When that husk is removed, the fruits look like a green tomato, which is why they're also called husk tomatoes.

IT TAKES TWO!

Tomatillos are very easy to grow, but they are not self-pollinating, and you need at least two plants for good fruit set. When planting, bury half of the stem beneath the soil to help encourage deep-rooting and drought-resistant plants. They are relatively low maintenance, but they do need 1 to 2 inches of water per week; too little water, and they will drop their blossoms without developing fruit.

It's not just the fruits that are larger; the plants of tomatillos are also bigger than those of Cape gooseberries and ground cherries. They can grow 3 to 4 feet tall and spread up to 3 feet across if left unsupported. I space my seedlings 2½ to 3 feet apart and stake them by placing three 4-foot stakes arranged in a triangle around each plant. I wrap garden twine around the supports as the plants grow to hold them in place.

BROWN HUSK = RIPE FRUIT

The fruits are ripe when the husks turn from green to brown. You can also give the husks a light squeeze to see if the fruits are firm and have filled out the wrapper. Once husked, you'll notice the skin on tomatillos has a sticky coating; just rinse it off before you use the fruit. Ripe tomatillos can be stored for up to 3 months by placing them in a single layer in a cool basement or room. However, the fruits can also be frozen (husk, rinse, dry, and freeze) in freezer bags. Any ripe fruits that are left on the ground will reseed the following spring and can be lifted and moved to a new spot or shared with tomatillo-loving friends.

GIVE PURPLE A WHIRL

Experimental gardeners (which I hope you are) will want to try purple tomatillos, which have very pretty purple-green fruits and a slightly sweeter taste than green tomatillos. If an early frost threatens, cover plants with a frost blanket or row cover to protect them, or pick the maturing fruit and allow them to continue ripening indoors. Full flavor is achieved when the fruits are mostly purple.

THE DETAILS

A.K.A.: Husk tomato, *Physalis ixocarpa*

DAYS TO MATURITY: 70–75 days

HAILS FROM: Central America

VARIETIES TO TRY: 'Toma Verde', purple

Purple
tomatillo

growing garden berries

> Grow Cape gooseberries, ground cherries, and tomatillos as you would tomatoes: start them
indoors 6 to 8 weeks before the last expected spring frost; plant them in a sunny garden
bed (or in big pots) with plenty of organic matter; water them regularly if there hasn't been rain;
and mulch them to suppress weeds, maintain soil moisture, and keep fruit clean.

> Garden berries all form protective, papery husks around their fruits, which help to discourage
bugs and birds. The plants are low maintenance, but they can fall prey to a handful of
pests, including cutworms, flea beetles, Colorado potato beetles, or striped cucumber beetles.
Be observant and take action where necessary. A lightweight row cover over the just-planted
seedlings will deter beetles. Remove when the plants begin to flower.

WHY GROW ORDINARY TOMATOES?

BEFORE CRAIG LeHOULLIER (author and tomato advisor to the Seed Savers Exchange) introduced me to the staggering assortment of colors, shapes, sizes, and flavors of heirloom tomatoes, I thought the sunny yellow fruits of 'Lemon Boy' were novel. Boy, was I in for a surprise! Soon I was picking the pea-size fruits of 'Mexico Midget', the weird clusters of 'Reisetomate', and the pale ivory tomatoes of 'Snow White'. *Note:* Days to harvest are from transplant, not direct seeding.

'BLACK ZEBRA' (80 days). Fruits of this cross between 'Green Zebra' and a black tomato have a remarkable sweet, smoky flavor. The 1½-inch tomatoes are burgundy-purple brushed with green streaks, and in my garden, they begin to ripen in August. The plants are indeterminate.

'CHOCOLATE SPRINKLES' (55 days). These grape-shaped tomatoes are super sweet with a unique color combination: red skin streaked with green stripes that combine to give a chocolaty appearance. The indeterminate plants are disease resistant and bear a heavy crop on long tresses.

'JAPANESE BLACK TRIFELE' (80 days). An heirloom with large pear-shaped fruits that are meaty and juicy. The flavor is complex; slightly smoky, with mild tones of balsamic vinegar. We love them for fresh eating, but they also make a delicious salsa and an amazing, and beautiful, caprese salad.

'MANDARIN CROSS' (80 days). My family is obsessed with orange tomatoes, and this golden Japanese slicer surpassed all expectation. The plants yield a heavy crop of medium-size, meaty fruits with a wonderful sweet flavor. Definitely a keeper.

'MEXICO MIDGET' (65 days). When Craig LeHoullier first told me about 'Mexico Midget', a pea-size heirloom with big tomato flavor, I thought he was pulling my leg. Then he kindly sent me some seed, and we've been growing them every year since. In fact, they reseed with abandon, so I just weed out excess seedlings each spring and leave a few to grow to maturity.

'REISETOMATE' (70 days). This one is just fun to grow: the large fruits look like clumps of cherry tomatoes stuck together. The lobes don't all ripen at the same time, a trait that earns 'Reisetomate' its nickname, traveler tomato — it could be taken on a journey and the individual bumps could be torn off as they ripen. It has a strong tomato flavor, thick skin, and a sometimes mealy texture.

'SNOW WHITE' (75 days). The past few summers, we've been enjoying the ivory yellow fruits of 'Snow White'. In fact, my tomato-loving niece has declared it her new favorite. The productive, indeterminate plants bear long clusters of Ping-Pong-ball–size tomatoes starting in midsummer.

'Snow White'

'Black Zebra'

'Chocolate Sprinkles'

'Japanese Black Trifele'

'Mandarin Cross'

'Mexico Midget'

'Reisetomate'

like peppers?

try these!

When I was growing up, I occasionally saw a red or green bell pepper pass through our kitchen, but I can't say I ate many of them. (As a very fussy kid, I'm sure that was mostly my fault.) When I finally got my own garden and started poring through seed catalogs, I quickly realized how many peppers there were just waiting for me to sample them. I wasn't interested in the common green or red peppers. I wanted the chocolate-colored peppers (Would they actually *taste* like chocolate? Nope!) and 'Sweet Banana' (the fruits actually do look like bananas!) and 'Chinese Five Color', which has plants that bear small peppers in a rainbow of colors all at the same time. Such diversity!

growing great peppers

> Peppers are a warm-season crop and need plenty of sunshine and warm, fertile, well-drained soil. Plant them in your sunniest garden beds, taking the time to prewarm the soil with black plastic 2 weeks before transplanting.

> Experience has shown me that getting peppers planted out sooner is not better. You can erect a mini hoop tunnel over your pepper bed to shelter the young seedlings, but if not, aim for a planting date that is 1 to 2 weeks after your last expected frost date.

> If you're in a short-summer region, grow peppers in containers on a paved driveway, where the dark asphalt will absorb heat and create a microclimate around them. In the garden, a greenhouse or poly tunnel will also extend the season in late summer and early autumn.

> Sweet peppers can be harvested while the fruits are full size but still green or when they've ripened to their mature color and peak sweetness. For hot peppers, wait to harvest until they look like the picture on the seed packet or in the seed catalog.

> When you harvest hot peppers, either wear gloves or wash your hands immediately afterward. I've rubbed my eyes too many times with peppery hands to not be vigilant about hand washing!

Uncommon Sweet Peppers You'll Love

FOR ME, SWEET PEPPERS ARE garden candy. As a novice gardener, I was hesitant to plant peppers, thinking them difficult to grow. How wrong I was! Given full sun and plenty of summer heat, peppers are very low maintenance and reliable. The first variety I tried was 'Sweet Banana', which charmed me with its bright yellow banana-shaped fruits. From there, I planted 'Purple Beauty' and 'Sweet Chocolate', enjoying the variety of colors and subtle flavor differences. *Note:* Days to harvest are from transplant, not direct seeding.

'SWEET CHOCOLATE' (78 days). Who can resist chocolate? Not me! So, when I saw 'Sweet Chocolate' listed in a seed catalog, and read that the plants are early producing and tolerant of cool weather, I knew I had to try them. Just 2 months from transplanting, we had medium-size green peppers; 2 to 3 weeks later, they ripened to that rich chocolate brown. The flavor was not chocolate sweet but peppery sweet and crunchy. The biggest fruits were about 3 inches long and 1½ inches at the shoulder, with fairly thin walls.

'PURPLE BEAUTY' (75 days). This was my first purple bell pepper, and it is one we continue to grow. The 18-inch-tall plants are reliable, even in our occasionally cool summers, and we all love the color. Compared to the modest size of 'Sweet Chocolate' peppers, these are large (3 to 4 inches long) three- or four-lobed, thick-walled peppers.

'SWEET BANANA' (75 days). My kids love the butter-yellow banana-shaped fruits of this award-winning heirloom. The 6- to 7-inch-long peppers will eventually ripen to red, but they can be picked at any stage. Their flavor is mild, but as the fruits turn red, they sweeten nicely. The plants are heavy producers, typically yielding around 20 peppers each.

'BIANCA' (65 days white, 85 days red). With most sweet peppers, the fruits start out green and eventually turn red, yellow, or orange as they mature. The fruits of 'Bianca', on the other hand, are pale ivory that ripen to a bright red. The plants are early to mature and produce a good yield of medium-size four-lobed peppers. 'Bianca' is also highly resistant to tobacco mosaic virus.

'CORNITO GIALLO' (55 days green, 75 days yellow). This is a 2016 All-America Selections variety that bears bull-horn-shaped fruits that grow 5 inches long and 1½ inches across at the shoulders. The plants are early to mature and yield a heavy crop of sweet, fruity peppers that emerge green but ripen to sunny yellow.

'CORBACI' (60 days green, 80 days red). If you're a pepper lover like me, you'll fall for 'Corbaci', an heirloom variety that yields clusters of long, slender fruits. Expect the peppers to grow 10 to 12 inches long but be less than an inch across. 'Corbaci' has a well-earned reputation for high production and can topple over when laden with fruits. Therefore, staking is recommended. The sweet fruits will mature from green to red.

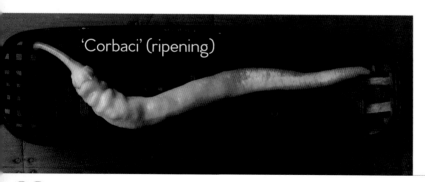

'Corbaci' (ripening)

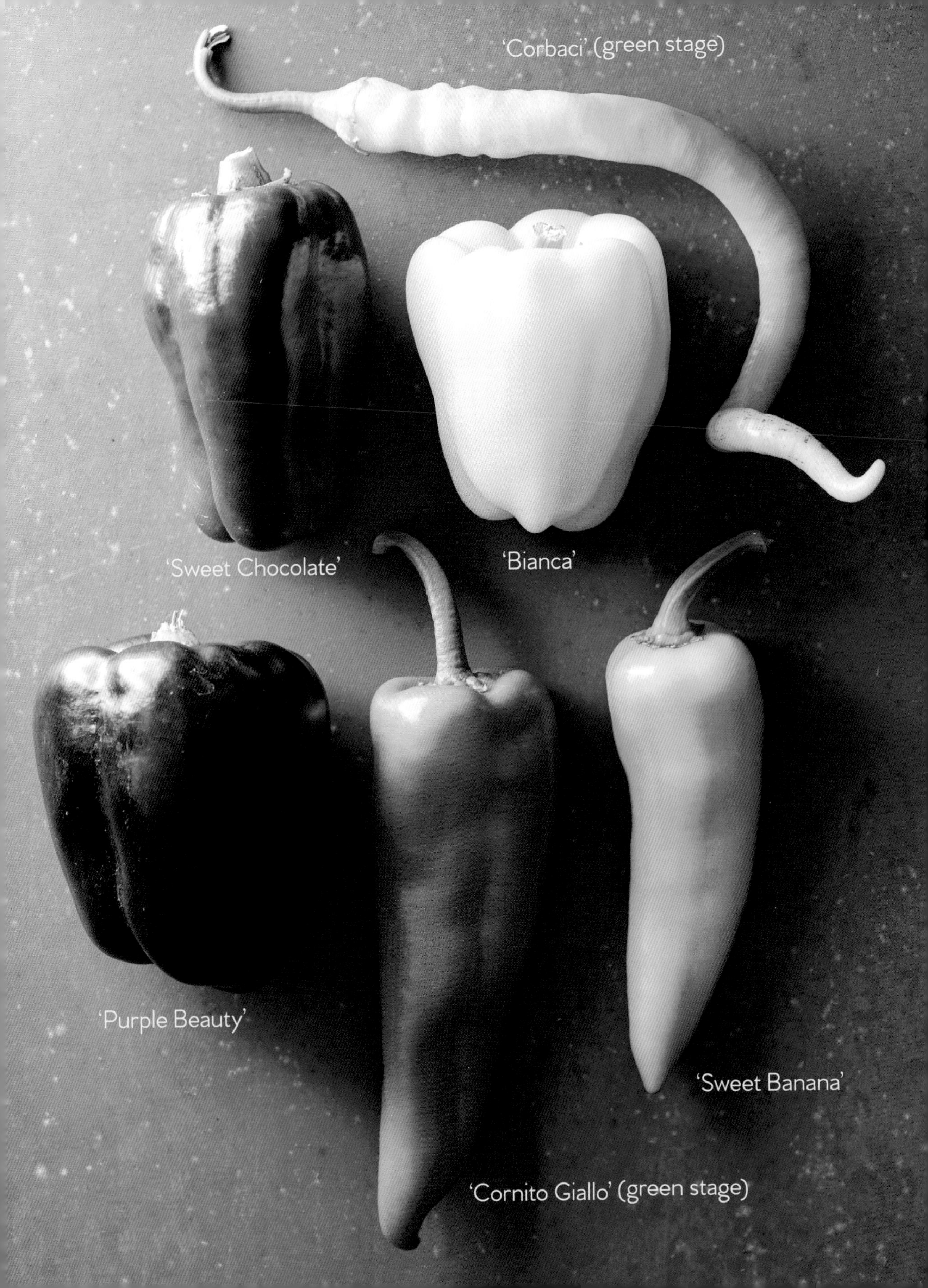

'Corbaci' (green stage)

'Sweet Chocolate'

'Bianca'

'Purple Beauty'

'Sweet Banana'

'Cornito Giallo' (green stage)

Uncommon Hot Peppers You'll Love

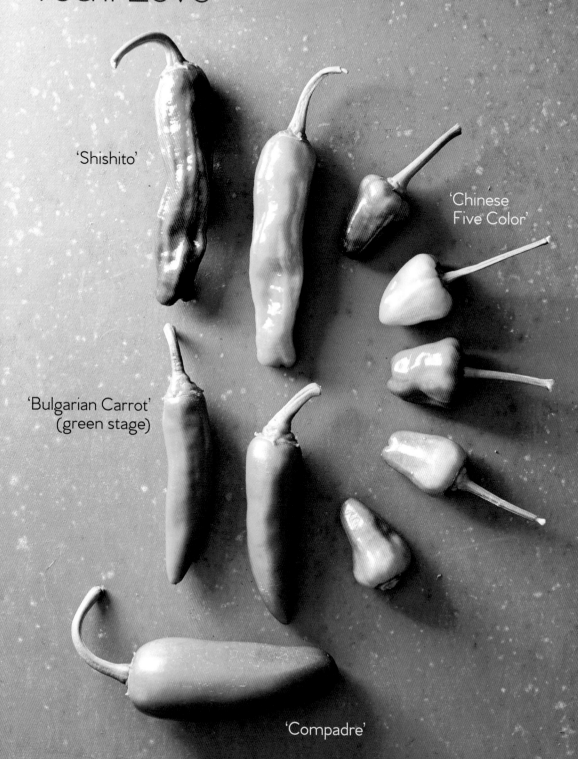

'Shishito'

'Chinese Five Color'

'Bulgarian Carrot' (green stage)

'Compadre'

EVEN NORTHERN GARDENERS like me can grow a bumper crop of hot peppers. Location is everything, so find your sunniest site; growing hot peppers in black plastic pots on my paved driveway works well for me. In the garden, I start them off with a mini hoop tunnel in early summer to trap heat and give them a good start. Next, select early-maturing varieties that will have time to ripen in your region. I've had great success with unique peppers like 'Chinese Five Color', 'Bulgarian Carrot', and 'Fish'. *Note:* Days to harvest are from transplant, not direct seeding.

'FISH' (80 days). This tasty hot pepper has beautiful green-and-white-streaked foliage and small (often striped!) peppers in hues of white, green, orange, and red. 'Fish' was introduced to the trade by heirloom vegetable expert William Woys Weaver, who notes that it was traditionally used in Baltimore as a substitute for paprika in cream sauces created for fish dishes. These peppers do pack quite a punch (think cayenne), but cooking will temper the heat somewhat.

'CHINESE FIVE COLOR' (70–90 days). I think the folks at Baker Creek Heirloom Seed Co. say it best: "Screaming hot little peppers that turn a rainbow of vibrant colors; from purple, cream, yellow, orange, to red as they ripen." The plants have purple-green foliage, and by midsummer they're smothered in the 1- to 2-inch-long fruits. The tiny peppers get hotter as they mature, so if you're spice shy, pick them while they're still purple.

'BULGARIAN CARROT' (75 days). At first glance, the long, tapered orange peppers on this variety look just like small carrots. But watch out, as they will bite you back!

The initial flavor of the ripened peppers is fruity, but it finishes hot — in the 5,000 to 30,000 Scoville range. The fruits grow 2 to 3½ inches long and are produced on 18-inch-tall plants.

'COMPADRE' (70 days). You might think this pepper looks just like any other jalapeño variety: bullet-shaped, about 4 inches long, with a glossy green that matures to bright red. But unlike other jalapeños, this one continues to flower in cool temperatures and can even withstand a light frost! This is a major selling point for short-season gardeners like me. 'Compadre' is also fairly high yielding and resistant to disease.

'SHISHITO' (60 days green, 75 days red). You could say that this Japanese variety is both a hot pepper *and* a sweet pepper. The 3-inch-long slightly crinkly peppers have a sweet flavor, but as the summer goes on, the heat increases — especially once the fruits mature to a ripe red. We love them grilled with a bit of olive oil and sea salt, but they're also amazing dipped in a tempura batter and flash-fried.

'BRAZILIAN STARFISH' (90 days). I suppose to some people the fruits of this variety do resemble their starfish namesakes, but to me they look more like miniature UFOs: they grow just 1½ to 2 inches wide but only an inch tall. Fruits start out bright green, eventually maturing to a vibrant lipstick red, and have thick walls, which give a nice, satisfying crunch when you bite into them. Their flavor is sweet and fruity, followed up by a blast of medium heat. These are tall, leggy plants that need to be staked or caged to keep them upright and off the ground.

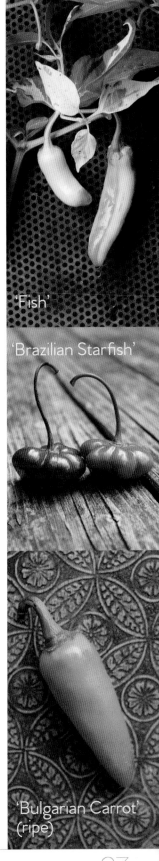

'Fish'

'Brazilian Starfish'

'Bulgarian Carrot' (ripe)

like cucumbers?

try these relatives!

'Palace King'

'Dragon's Egg'

'Poona Kheera'

'Boothby's Blonde'

'Mini White'

'Hmong Red'
(immature)

Cucamelon
with flower

'Suyo Long'

Crisp, crunchy cucamelons
are delicious, easy to grow,
and incredibly productive.
Their cucumber-like flavor is
punctuated with a citrus twist,
hence their alias, Mexican
sour gherkin.

Our family *loves* trying different kinds of cucumbers. Each summer, our cucumber beds are planted with at least a dozen species and varieties, but few look like "traditional" cucumbers. As you walk the pathways between the beds, you might notice the slender twisted fruits of 'Painted Serpent' hiding beneath a mound of foliage, or the weird kiwi-shaped fruits of 'Little Potato' climbing an A-frame trellis. You'll also see some of the more popular heirloom cucumbers, like 'Lemon', 'Crystal Apple', 'Boothby's Blonde', and 'Poona Kheera'. And you'll definitely find one that isn't related but nonetheless tastes like a cucumber — the cucamelon! All three of my nieces have birthdays within a 2-week span in late summer, and every year, they all ask for the same gift — a big container of cucamelons.

Not all cucumbers live up to their hype (true for any vegetable); we've tried many that we've found disappointing or simply not to our liking. But that's part of the fun of having a vegetable garden — experimenting! Here are a few cucumbers (and cucumber-*like* plants) we've tried and loved.

TRY THIS!
Cute, Crunchy Cucamelons

WHAT'S THE MOST POPULAR CROP in our vegetable garden? Easy! It's cucamelon. The fruits, which look *exactly* like tiny watermelons, rarely make it into the kitchen; instead, we gobble them up by the handful, straight from the vines. The plant is a distant relative of cucumbers, and these inch-long fruits do have a cucumber-like flavor with a pleasing citrus tang.

Very rarely, you might find cucamelons at the farmers' market, but they can fetch up to $20 a pound! The price alone makes them worth growing for yourself. They're an easy crop; the vines are very productive, and they're rarely troubled by the many insects and diseases that plague cucumbers.

SLOW TO START, BUT VIGOROUS

Impatient gardeners will find cucamelons slow to start in the garden, with growth not taking off until the summer weather heats up. That said, they will tolerate a cooler spring better than cucumbers do, and once they're established, cucamelons are quite a bit more drought tolerant. The vines are delicate looking, with thin stems and small leaves, but don't be fooled! This is a plant that can hold its own in the garden. People with limited growing space can plant them in large pots on a deck or patio; just be sure to provide something for the vigorous vines to climb.

SOURS WITH AGE

About a week after you see the first flowers, begin checking for ripe cucamelons. They tend to hide behind the foliage, so look closely. Once they're about an inch long, start picking. The sourness of the skin intensifies as the fruits age, so pick them young if you want to minimize the citrus bite. We start picking the first fruits in late July or early August, with the last few plucked from the vines in October.

Cucamelons are open-pollinated and produce both male and female flowers on the same plant, so you can save the seed from any ripe fruits that fall to the ground. Warm-climate gardeners will find that a few cucamelons left behind will self-seed quite easily.

There are so many ways to use these fun fruits. As the name suggests, they're perfect for pickling! We eat them out of hand, pack them in the kids' lunch boxes, and take them along to picnics and barbecues. You could even pop them into your gin and tonic.

THE DETAILS

A.K.A.: Mexican sour gherkin, mouse melon, *Melothria scabra*

DAYS TO MATURITY: 75 days from direct seeding

HAILS FROM: Mexico and Central America

VARIETIES TO TRY: None

growing great cucumbers and cucumber melons

> Start the seeds indoors 6 weeks before your last spring frost. Sow the seed in 4-inch pots to give the plants a chance to develop a substantial root system before planting out and to minimize transplant shock. Once the risk of frost has passed, harden off the young plants and move them to the garden.

> Gardeners in northern regions with unpredictable late-spring weather may wish to protect young plants with cloches or a mini hoop tunnel. Open the ends of the tunnel during the day to regulate temperature and allow air to circulate. I usually leave the mini tunnel in place for 2 to 3 weeks, depending on how quickly summer arrives, then replace it with a trellis.

> Heat, sun, and rich soil are the keys to growing success with these plants, so pick a site with full sun and amend the soil with aged manure or compost.

> Seriously consider trellising the plants. We grow ours on sturdy A-frame trellises; this keeps the foliage and fruit off the ground, which minimizes the risk of diseases and makes harvesting a snap. Also, unsupported plants will sprawl in every direction, quickly taking over a garden bed.

> If you want to save the seeds of heirloom cucumbers and cucumber-like plants, such as burr cucumber, just let a few fruits ripen fully on the vines, or collect any fallen fruits at the end of summer. Scoop out the seeds, which will be surrounded by a gel-like coating, and place them in a container, along with a small amount of water. Leave the mixture to ferment for 3 days (expect mold to form on the surface). The good seeds will sink to the bottom of the container; when this happens, pour off the mold, pulp, and water. Rinse the seeds left at the bottom of the container with fresh water until clean. Spread them on paper towels or a clean dishcloth and let dry for at least a week. Store the fully dried seeds in envelopes.

West Indian
burr gherkin

THE DETAILS

A.K.A.: Burr cucumber, *Cucumis anguria*

DAYS TO MATURITY: 70 days

HAILS FROM: West Africa

VARIETIES TO TRY: None

TRY THIS!
West Indian Burr Gherkin

AT FIRST GLANCE, the spine-covered fruits of West Indian burr gherkin don't look very appetizing. But they actually have a remarkably pleasant crunch and a sweet, cucumber-like flavor. The trick is to pick the fruits young, when they're just an inch or two long and the spines are still soft. The plants are very easy to grow, vigorous, and relatively free of pests and diseases. Plus, the watermelon-like foliage, bright yellow blooms, and spiky egg-shaped fruits are very striking, making this a fun choice for an ornamental edible in a flower garden, children's plot, or a space next to a deck or patio.

Although its name implies a Caribbean origin, culinary historian William Woys Weaver points out that it is actually West African. The seed was introduced to the United States by Minton Collins of Virginia. Collins's seed was obtained from Jamaica, and the "new" vegetable eventually became known as the West Indian burr gherkin. However, when its lineage was traced further back, it was discovered to have come from West Africa and was brought to Jamaica during the slave trade.

MONSTER VINES

Small-space gardeners be warned: burr cucumbers aren't shy about putting on growth. You can expect the vines to grow 8 to 10 feet long. If allowed to sprawl on the ground, they will quickly conquer a 4- by 10-foot garden bed. Save space by trellising the plants on a sturdy, wooden A-frame trellis; this will keep the plants under control and make harvesting easier. The plants do produce tendrils, but they're not as vertically inclined as cucumbers are, so they need a little help when climbing. Tie up the new shoots as they grow. Wear gloves for this task, as the foliage is also covered in tiny spines.

If you have the space to let the vines run across the ground, mulch with straw to keep the leaves and fruits clean. The good news is that you won't have to worry much about weeds; the vines' dense growth will choke out all but the most persistent weeds. Burr cucumbers are also very drought tolerant and thrive in hot weather. If there has been no rain, a weekly watering will keep production high, as will a monthly dose of a liquid fish or seaweed solution or a balanced organic fertilizer.

PICK 'EM SMALL

Begin harvesting the oval fruits when they're just ¾ inch long. At this stage, the burrs are soft and the skin is quite thin. You can simply pop the whole fruit in your mouth or gather enough to pickle. Although the young fruits are quite a treat, if you let them mature, those spikes will firm up and the flesh will turn seedy and bitter. If you prefer, scrape off the burrs with a knife, or place the fruit in a dish towel and rub to quickly and easily remove the spikes.

You'll also want to keep on top of the harvest, removing any overmature fruits. If burr cucumbers are left to mature on the vines, the plant will switch from fruit to seed production and the harvest will come to an end. If you'd like to maintain a steady supply of the fruit, sow a second crop 4 to 6 weeks after the initial planting.

'Mandurian Round'

TRY THIS!
Cucumber Melons

QUESTION: What looks like a cucumber, grows like a cucumber, tastes like a cucumber, but isn't a cucumber?

Answer: Cucumber melons! Botanically, these are muskmelons, but because they resemble cucumbers and have a similar flavor, they are typically sold as cucumbers in seed catalogs and at farmers' markets. There are two main botanical varieties of cucumber melons: *Cucumis melo* var. *flexuosus*, which includes snake melons like 'Painted Serpent', and *Cucumis melo* var. *adzhur*, which are often called Italian cucumbers.

I was first introduced to these uncommon fruits about 10 years ago when, on impulse, I added a packet of Armenian cucumber seed to my early-spring seed order. At the time, I wasn't sure they would grow in my cool climate, but I knew that they were a popular crop in the Middle East and I wanted to try growing them for my Lebanese in-laws.

By late July, we had our first cucumber. The seed packet said the fruits can grow up to 2 feet long, but we picked it when it was about 10 inches. We couldn't wait any longer! The pale green fruit was deeply ridged and covered in soft fuzz — just beautiful. The skin was thin and didn't need to be peeled, so we sliced up the melon and enjoyed it in the garden. The flesh was very crisp and mild tasting, with an almost sweet, cucumber flavor. We were hooked!

Since that initial harvest, I've become quite a fan of cucumber melons and am always on the lookout for varieties we haven't yet tried. There is quite a diversity of

A.K.A.: *Cucumis melo*

DAYS TO MATURITY: 60–70 days from transplant

HAILS FROM: Middle East into South Asia

VARIETIES TO TRY: 'Painted Serpent', Armenian cucumber, 'Mandurian Round'

fruit sizes, shapes, and colors, with some, like 'Carosello Tonda di Fasano', producing round green fruits, and others, like 'Painted Serpent', that produce slender striped fruits.

KEEP THE LEAVES DRY

Cucumber melons can be grown on the ground, but generally, you can expect healthier plants and cleaner, straighter fruits when they are grown vertically. The exceptions are the compact, nonvining types, such as 'Mandurian Round' and 'Carosello Barese'.

Cucumber melons can be susceptible to diseases like powdery mildew, so take care when watering and avoid wetting the leaves, which can spread disease. Water only the base of the plants. If powdery mildew is an annual issue in your garden, consider applying a baking soda spray weekly. (See page 43 for a recipe.) To encourage healthy growth and a large harvest, fertilize plants every 2 to 3 weeks with a liquid organic fertilizer, such as fish emulsion or liquid kelp.

PICK EARLY, PICK OFTEN

Because these are melons, not cucumbers, you can expect them to take longer to bear fruit. We typically harvest our first cucumber melon in late July, with the harvest extending into late September.

Harvest and eat cucumber melons when they are immature. They do size up quickly once fruits are formed, however, so keep a close eye on the garden, and pick when they have reached a harvestable size. Don't allow them to stay on the vine, as quality and flavor will decline. The fruits will also become seedier.

GROW THESE!

Here are some of my family's favorite cucumber melons.

'PAINTED SERPENT' (70 days). These are also called yard-long cucumbers, snake melons, or as my Lebanese mother-in-law knows them, *metki*. The name "painted serpent" comes from the curious appearance of the fruit, which are long and slender and boldly striped in alternating shades of light and dark green. If allowed to grow on the ground, they curl and twist among the foliage, like a snake ready to strike. The fruits will grow up to 30 inches long but are best harvested when they are 8 to 16 inches long.

ARMENIAN CUCUMBER (70 days). This was my first introduction to cucumber melons, and we continue to grow it because its fruits have outstanding quality and flavor, and because the plants are so productive. The ribbed fruits make beautiful slices on a plate, resembling flowers. Plus, the soft green color makes it easy to spot the fruits among the dense dark green foliage. Harvest when fruits are 8 to 12 inches in length. They will grow up to 2 feet long, but eating quality seriously declines at their mature size.

'MANDURIAN ROUND' (65 days). Like Armenian cukes, this variety also produces pale green fuzzy, ribbed melons. Instead of being oblong, though, these are adorable almost-round fruits. The plants also have different growth habits. Whereas Armenian cucumbers yield long vines, 'Mandurian Round' bears its fruit on squat semi-bush plants. Expect them to grow no more than 5 feet in length. The fruits, however, can get quite large — up to 10 inches in diameter — but are at their peak when picked at 3 to 4 inches. The soft fuzz rubs off easily with a dishcloth or under running water.

Armenian
cucumber

WHY GROW ORDINARY CUCUMBERS?

As we began to explore and expand our global garden, I quickly realized just how many different types and varieties of cucumbers were available to gardeners. Unlike tomatoes, which are celebrated in festivals, events, and tastings across North America, cucumbers get no fanfare and no celebrations. It's true that they don't have the breadth of flavors that you find with tomatoes, but I'd go to a cucumber festival any day! Their color range runs from pale white to deep rusty brown, with shades of gold, yellow, amber, and every tone of green tucked in between. And yes, there are subtle flavor differences. When you're ready to plan your own cucumber festival, start with some of the outstanding varieties below.

'Poona Kheera'

very mature

mature

'Boothby's Blonde'

mature

very mature

Intriguing Indian Cucumbers

AS I PULLED OUR FIRST MATURE 'Poona Kheera' cucumber from the vine, I held it up to show the kids. "What do you think?" I asked. "Weird" was their answer. Admittedly, it is a rather unusual-looking cucumber. Its large football-shaped fruits have reddish brown skin that looks as if it's been painted with a crackle finish. The important question, though, wasn't "How does it look?" but rather "How does it taste?" So we sliced it up. "Amazing!" said the kids. And just like that, we fell in love with Indian cucumbers.

Indian cucumbers are true cucumbers, which are believed to have originated in Southern Asia, somewhere between the Bay of Bengal and the rugged Himalayas. As I learned with 'Poona Kheera', the shapes and colors of Indian cucumbers may be unfamiliar, but their flavors are outstanding.

Indian cucumbers are later to mature than typical North American cucumber varieties but are grown in much the same way. For best results, follow the growing instructions for cucumber melons (see page 28).

'POONA KHEERA' (55–60 days). This Indian cucumber is popular for its early maturity, ease of cultivation, and high production. Most gardeners harvest the ovoid-shaped fruits when immature and pale yellow, but even the mature fruits are tasty!

As they ripen, the skin turns brownish red, eventually turning golden brown with a russet potato–like netting covering the surface. Surprisingly, they're still delicious when they reach this stage. The flesh is white and dense enough to stand up to a quick turn on the barbecue or be made into a crisp cucumber salad without wilting or turning to mush.

'LITTLE POTATO' (70 days). Personally, I think 'Little Potato' (also sold as 'Khira Balam') looks more like a kiwi than a potato, but either way, it's a fun variety and has become a favorite in our garden. The plants have a semi-bush habit and are extremely productive, making them a good choice for gardeners with limited space. The fruits are smaller and rounder than 'Poona Kheera' but have the same mature rusty-brown coloring and crackly skin. The pale green flesh is sweet with an undertone of citrus and stays crisp for a very long time.

'SIKKIM' (70 days). This variety has the exotic netted, reddish brown skin of many Indian cucumbers, but these fruits can grow large — almost as large as a football! — and can weigh several pounds. Of course, they're best picked before that stage, when they're about 6 inches long. Like many heirlooms, these are grown for their flavor and texture (mildly sweet, dense, crisp flesh) and aren't as productive as certain newer hybrids.

'Poona Kheera'

'Sikkim' (immature)

White Cucumbers for Less Bitterness

AS A RULE, I find white cucumbers to be crisper and less bitter than typical green slicing varieties. Of course, not all of these are *true* white, with most leaning more toward ivory, milky green, or soft yellow. However, they all have excellent flavor and a dense, crisp texture. The fruits of white varieties are also easier to spot among the dense foliage, especially when grown on the ground.

'CRYSTAL APPLE' (75 days). 'Crystal Apple' was introduced to North America almost a century ago by an Australian seed company, and it has its origins in China. It's a great pick for children, who love to hunt for the pale green, kiwi-shaped fruits. For the highest-quality cucumbers, harvest them when they're still light in color and less than 3 inches long. One warning: the stem end of the fruit can become bitter if the plants are not evenly and regularly irrigated.

'LEMON' (68 days). These crunchy little cukes were my introduction to heirloom vegetables, and they remain one of my favorite cucumbers to grow and eat. The flavor is mild and the lovely light-green-and-yellow-streaked skin is very thin; no peeling required! The long vines are incredibly productive. I've found them to be more resistant to common cucumber diseases, like powdery mildew and rust, than other popular varieties. Pick the fruits before they turn bright yellow, and rub off the thin spines before eating.

'BOOTHBY'S BLONDE' (63 days). Here's a cucumber worth saving! At least, that's what the Slow Food organization thinks; it has identified 'Boothby's Blonde' as a variety in need of preserving and has included it in its Ark of Taste. I'd have to agree! The pale green fruits are about 4 inches long and have a delicious sweet snap to them.

'DRAGON'S EGG' (65 days). We've only been growing this fun little heirloom for a few years, but it quickly earned "family favorite" status and is now an annual crop in our garden. The vines are cucumber factories, pumping out dozens of the 3- to 5-inch-long, egg-shaped fruits. The cream-colored skin is smooth and thin, and they have a smaller seed cavity than 'Lemon' cucumbers. The fun name, egg shape, and crisp, mild flavor have made it a big hit with the kids!

'Boothby's Blonde' (seed-saving stage)

'Boothby's Blonde'

'Dragon's Egg'

'Crystal Apple'

'Lemon'

'Hmong Red'
(immature)

'Suyo Long'

'Palace King'

TRY THIS!
Amazing Asian Cucumbers

ASIAN CUCUMBERS ARE often long and slender, growing up to 24 inches long, but only 1½ to 2 inches in diameter. The fruits can be bumpy or spiny but are typically bitter-free and considered to be "burpless": easier to digest and milder tasting. To get that long, straight fruit, however, you'll need to trellis your plants or grow them up a fence.

'SUYO LONG' (60–65 days). I was first introduced to this traditional Chinese variety through Annapolis Seeds, one of my local heirloom-seed companies. The temptation of long, slim bitter-free cucumbers that twist and curl when grown on the ground was too much to resist. Soon after planting, the vines crawled up our trellises and over the ground, as they headed off in the direction of our neighbor's house. By early August, the first cucumbers were ready to pick and, as promised, they were crisp and sweet with no hint of bitterness. The fruits grow up to 18 inches long, but we try to pick them when they're at their peak and less than 1 foot in length.

'PALACE KING' (60 days). Like many Asian cucumbers, 'Palace King' is easy to grow and produces long, narrow fruits. However, they are usually picked smaller than other varieties: when just 8 to 10 inches long. They have thin skin with little bumps and white spines (which are easily wiped off). The vines are extremely productive and should be trellised if you want perfectly straight cucumbers.

'HMONG RED' (60–65 days). Not so much red but more of a rusty orange at maturity, these large oval fruits certainly walk on the wild side of the garden. The large vines produce an abundance of fruits, some of which may be up to 1 foot long and about 3 to 4 inches wide. The flavor is mild and forms the base for a simple summer treat I learned about from the folks at Baker Creek Heirloom Seeds: Split a cucumber in half lengthwise. Use a spoon to scrape out and discard the seeds, then use a fork to scrape the flesh into a bowl. Add a spoonful of sugar, mix well, and enjoy! It's a refreshing way to cool down on a hot summer day.

wanted: achocha

Achocha, also known as the Bolivian cucumber or slipper gourd (*Cyclanthera brachystachya*), is at the top of my "gotta get" list. The slipper-shaped fruits, which are said to have a cucumber flavor, are produced on lengthy vines and can be eaten raw or cooked.

like summer squash?

try edible gourds!

It was the surprise of learning that my beautiful long cucuzza gourds were edible (see page 1) that prompted me to delve more into the world of edible gourds. There are many others that can be grown as a food crop, but these are my favorites and the ones that I find most reliable in my garden. Their flavor and texture compare extremely well to summer squash, so you can use them in your favorite squash and zucchini recipes. But I would also suggest you experiment with how they are cooked in other parts of the world, like India, Thailand, Japan, China, and the Middle East. Just remember to pick them while they're still immature!

growing edible gourds

> Most gourds need a long, warm season to grow and mature, so start the seeds indoors 5 to 6 weeks before your expected last frost date.

> Gourd germination is low and slow: If half of my seeds germinate, I feel like I've won the botanical lottery. I've had seeds germinate in as little as a week, but sometimes it takes as long as a month. Generally, 10 to 14 days is typical.

> You can speed up germination by using a nail file to clip the ends of the hard seed coat or run the seeds along medium-grit sandpaper. Soaking the seeds for 24 hours before planting will also help; I soak my clipped or sanded seeds in a plastic baggie filled with wet paper towels. Plant soaked seeds in 4-inch pots and place them in a warm spot to germinate; the top of the fridge is fine, but if you have a seedling heat mat, go ahead and use it.

> Once the danger of frost has passed and the seedlings are hardened off, transplant them to a site with full sun and rich soil. I amend the soil with rotted manure or compost, but I also follow that up with a monthly dose of liquid kelp to maintain a steady supply of nutrients. Avoid high-nitrogen fertilizers, as they will encourage leaves, not fruits.

> Edible gourds produce very long vigorous vines that need strong structures to climb. I use wooden A-frame trellises, but you can grow them up any sturdy fence, pergola, arbor, or other structure that will allow them to climb.

> Most gourds benefit from hand-pollination. The easiest way to do this is to pick a male flower, remove the petals, and gently press the pollen against a female flower (the one with the tiny fruit under the bloom). One male flower will pollinate up to five female flowers. Early evening is the best time to hand-pollinate.

> Once planted, gourds are quick to grow and bothered by few insects or diseases, but I have found powdery mildew to be an occasional issue. To discourage it, water early in the day and avoid wetting the leaves. I also spray every 10 to 14 days with a homemade baking soda solution: 1 tablespoon of baking soda, 1 teaspoon of vegetable oil (or dormant oil), and 1 teaspoon of liquid soap to a gallon of water. Mix well and spray, coating the tops and bottoms of the leaves.

Edible snake gourds, nestled among their nonedible relatives.

TRY THIS!
Bottle Gourds

THE DETAILS

A.K.A.: *Lagenaria siceraria*

DAYS TO MATURITY: 70–80 days

HAILS FROM: Africa

VARIETIES TO TRY: Cucuzza, calabash

ALTHOUGH NOT WIDELY GROWN by home gardeners (perhaps because they're not a common kitchen vegetable?), edible gourds are definitely worth planting. They're super easy to grow, insect and disease resistant, and very productive. You'll need to give the vining plants plenty of space to sprawl or a sturdy structure to climb. Expect the vines to grow 8 to 12 feet long, but given ample organic matter and full sun, they can reach lengths over 20 feet!

BEST BOTTLE GOURDS

Our family has tried our share of bottle gourds! Here are the ones we like best.

CUCUZZA. If you read the introduction to this book, you'll know that a large part of my early inspiration for my global vegetable garden came from my experience growing cucuzze for my in-laws. Sometimes referred to as snake gourds, they're actually different from *true* snake gourds (*Trichosanthes cucumerina* var. *anguina*; see page 46) in both flavor and appearance. To ensure a heavy crop of cucuzze, I hand-pollinate the female blooms in the evening as they open. Soon we are picking those gorgeous soft green, elongated fruits when they are at their peak of quality, 8 to 12 inches long. For fun, we always let a few grow to maturity — reaching lengths up to 4½ feet. It takes months to dry them indoors, but when they are fully dried, they can be painted or used as autumn decor.

Cucuzza plants also offer a harvest of *tenerumi* (as they're called in Sicily): the vine ends with the tendrils still attached. These are harvested when they're about 6 inches long, either fried in olive oil or steamed, and served simply as a green.

CALABASH. There are many varieties of calabash, also called opo, long squash, or simply bottle gourd. Some have squat green fruits, others are extralong, with a few even growing in flat, round shapes. The variety 'Long Opo' produces pale green cylindrical fruits that should be harvested when they are around a foot in length and 2 to 3 inches in diameter. They're quick to grow (ready in about 75 days) and have mild, white flesh with hints of sweetness. Calabash gourds can be cooked in all the same ways as summer squash.

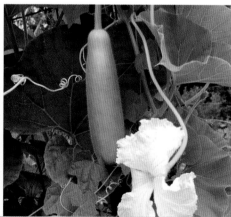

'Long Opo'
calabash

THE DETAILS

A.K.A.: Serpent gourd, padwal, *Trichosanthes cucumerina* var. *anguina*

DAYS TO MATURITY: 70–80 days

HAILS FROM: South Asia

VARIETIES TO TRY: 'Buag Ngu', 'Snaky'

TRY THIS!
Snake Gourds

MOST PEOPLE GROW SNAKE GOURDS for their namesake long dark-green-and-white striped fruits, but I also like to grow them for their flowers, which are among the most beautiful and intricate blossoms I've ever seen. The buds don't unfurl until the sun sets, and as they open, they reveal exotic-looking creamy white blooms that are surrounded by long, lacy tendrils. Bonus: they're deeply fragrant. This after-hours show is for the pollinating moths, who I hope appreciate it as much as I do. However, I find the best crop comes when I give those moths a helping hand, so I hand-pollinate whenever I see newly opened female flowers.

The shape of the fruits can be quite variable. Those produced by the variety 'Buag Ngu' are squat, but the fruits of 'Snaky' (a type that is adaptable to many different growing conditions) can grow up to 18 inches long. Harvest the short-fruited snake gourds when they are 6 to 8 inches long and the long varieties when they are 15 to 18 inches. Snake gourds can be cooked like zucchini, but they are also spectacular when pickled or chopped into chutney or curry.

Luffa Gourds

HERE'S AN INTERESTING VEGETABLE!
When it's mature, you can use it to scrub down in the shower, but when it's young and tender, you can eat it. The flavor of the young fruits is similar to summer squash, and they can be cooked in the same way: roasted, stir-fried, stuffed, added to curry, or layered with cheese and tomato sauce in a savory parmigiana. You can even eat the very young fruits raw!

There are two main types of luffa: ridged (*Luffa acutangula*) and smooth, or common (*L. cylindrica*). Both can be eaten young or allowed to mature for their unusual sponges. If you can't decide which type to grow for eating, opt for the ridged luffa, which is generally thought to have superior flavor.

PRETTY BUT BOSSY
These are very ornamental plants, producing clusters of large yellow male and female flowers all summer long. If you give pollination a helping hand (see page 43), these will be followed by elongated fruits. Like most gourds, the vines are vigorous (translation: "absolutely ridiculously rampant plants that are trying to take over the world"). You have been forewarned. Give them a fence or something very sturdy to climb.

FRUITS FOR THE KITCHEN OR THE SHOWER
For edible fruits, pick baby luffa gourds when they're just 2 to 3 inches long or slightly larger. But be sure to harvest them before they reach 6 inches in length, at which point they become fibrous and unpalatable.

If you want sponges, let a few fruits grow to their mature size, up to 2 feet in length. In warmer regions, the fruits will ripen and dry on the vine. In my garden, I harvest the luffas when they are mature and the green skin has turned yellowish and bring them indoors to finish drying (a process that takes 2 to 3 weeks). Once the skin is brown and hard, use a hammer to crack one end of the fruit and shake out the seeds for future harvests. Then soak the gourds in a pan of water overnight to soften the skin for easy peeling, which reveals the unique spongy interior.

The fruits of the luffa gourd are a tasty treat when picked young, but once they grow longer than 6 inches, eating quality declines and they're best saved for dried sponges.

THE DETAILS

A.K.A.: Loofa, dishcloth gourd, Chinese okra, vegetable sponge, *Luffa cylindrica*, *L. acutangula*

DAYS TO MATURITY: 80–90 days for edible fruits, 110–50 days for sponges

HAILS FROM: South Asia

VARIETIES TO TRY: Smooth luffa: 'Dok', 'Edible Ace'

Ridged luffa (a.k.a. Chinese okra): 'Bonzana'

WHY GROW ORDINARY SUMMER SQUASHES?

'Bennings Green Tint'

'Costata Romanesca'

'Golden Dawn'

Cousa

'Eight Ball'

'Sunburst'

TRADITIONAL GARDENING ADVICE: "You only need one, maybe two zucchini plants."

Me: "Umm, okay, but how can I be expected to choose just one or two varieties when there are hundreds offering a mind-blowing assortment of fruit colors, shapes, and, yes, even flavors?"

The answer, of course, is that I don't. I grow at least a dozen varieties each summer, including our handful of family favorites, as well as new hybrids and new-to-me heirlooms. We use and freeze as much as we can during the growing season, and the extras are gobbled up by family, friends, unsuspecting neighbors, and the local food bank.

For a brief glimpse into the diversity of summer squash, let me introduce you to a few of the many types available through seed catalogs. In addition to green or yellow zucchini, there are Italian heirlooms like 'Costata Romanesco' and 'Tromboncino', Middle Eastern cousa, crookneck, scallop, globe, and odd-shaped ones like 'Lemon' (seriously adorable). My mother loves the scalloped edge and flattened shape of pattypan squash, while my mother-in-law prefers the light green speckled fruits of cousa, which she stuffs with meat, rice, and spices. Me? I love them all.

COUSA (50 days). Among the best-tasting types of summer squash, cousa types have thin pale green, speckled skin and an oblong, almost oval shape. We love their firm texture and mildly nutty flavor. Best varieties include 'Lebanese White Bush Marrow', 'Clarinette', 'Alexandria', and 'Magda'.

TATUME (60–65 days). This Mexican squash can be harvested young, as a summer squash (but sweeter!), or allowed to

Tatume

immature

mature

'Sunburst' pattypan

'Tromboncino'

Crookneck

oil), but they're also great pan-fried or roasted. Bigger fruits can be hollowed out as a vessel for soup or stuffed and baked. Best varieties include 'Flying Saucer', 'Sunburst', 'Benning's Green Tint', 'Lunar Eclipse', 'Moonbeam', and 'Jaune et Vert'.

ROUND (50–55 days). Round zucchini are extremely popular among market growers as well as gardeners because they are early to produce and remarkably prolific, especially if harvested regularly. They have a firm texture and a flavor that hints of nuts and butter. We love to slice off the top and stuff them with rice, meat, vegetables, and spices, but they can also be roasted whole, barbecued, or stir-fried. Best varieties include 'Ronde de Nice', 'Eight Ball', 'Floridor', 'Summer Ball', and the roundish varieties 'Papaya Pear' and 'Lemon'.

CROOKNECK (60 days). Plan to harvest when just 6 or 7 inches long; these attractive fruits have rounded bottoms and curved (or crooked) necks. Best varieties include 'Yellow Crookneck', 'Early Summer', 'Early Golden', and 'Zephyr', which is a bit of a straight crookneck but has unique golden fruits with funny green bottoms.

'TROMBONCINO' (70 days for summer squash, 90 days for winter squash). Also called rampicante, trumpet or serpentine squash, the slender, curving fruits of this Italian heirloom are as beautiful as they are delicious. The 1½ to 3 foot fruits are produced on long vines. We train them up A-frame trellises to encourage straight fruits. If allowed to sprawl on the ground, they will twist into gently curved shapes. Eat the pale green squash as a tender summer vegetable, or allow them to mature for an outstanding winter squash.

mature into a winter-type squash. Unlike most summer squash, tatume grows on vines that are best described as "aggressive" and will quickly reach 10 feet or more. The fruits are round to oblong in shape with deep green, striped, and speckled skin. To harvest as a summer squash, pick the fruits when they are the size of softballs. Mature fruits will grow to about 8 inches in diameter by the end of the summer and can be prepared as you would winter squash.

SCALLOP or PATTYPAN SQUASH (55–60 days). My kids call these UFOs, based on their flattened shape and scalloped edges. I just think they're fun to grow *and* fun to eat! We pick them when they're a scant 2 to 3 inches across for barbecuing whole (brushed with garlic-infused olive

growing great squash

> Summer and winter squash can be direct-seeded as soon as the risk of frost has passed. Or, give them a head start indoors, sowing seeds 3 to 4 weeks before the last expected frost. To speed up germination of direct seeded squash and encourage an extra-early crop, prewarm the soil for 2 weeks by placing black plastic mulch on garden beds.

> Give squash plants full sun and plenty of organic matter; they are nutrient pigs. I dig in at least 3 inches of aged manure or compost. If your manure isn't well aged, don't use it; too much nitrogen will encourage very healthy squash plants but few flowers and fruits.

> Squash can be grown in beds or hills. For hill planting, sow four or five seeds per hill, spacing the hills 4 feet apart. Thin to the strongest two plants.

> Summer squash are very quick to grow — usually just 7 weeks from seed to harvest — and therefore can be succession planted for a steady supply of high-quality fruits. Winter squash are a long season crop and are planted at the same time as summer squash in late spring, but won't be ready to harvest until early autumn.

> Summer squash are warm-season vegetables that usually grow on bush-type plants. There are a few exceptions to this rule — like 'Tromboncino' (see page 50) — an Italian vining variety, which is best grown on an A-frame trellis to save space, keep the foliage clean, and reduce the occurrence of powdery mildew. Winter squash can be produced on bush, semi-bush or vining plants. The vining types take up a lot of space and will need plenty of room to run.

> Covering just-seeded squash beds with an insect cover or lightweight row cover will reduce infestations of squash bugs, squash vine borer, and striped cucumber beetles. Remove the cover when flowers appear, as they need to be pollinated to produce fruits. Continue to handpick pests.

> All types of summer squash benefit from being harvested while still young: 6 to 8 inches for zucchini types, 2 to 3 inches across for pattypan and globe types, 4 to 6 inches for cousa types, 12 to 15 inches for 'Tromboncino'. Winter squash are ready to pick when the skin has turned its mature color and the rind is hard. Harvest before frost.

like winter squash?

W hat's your favorite way to warm up on a cold winter day? Mine is to put on a big pot of homemade squash soup! With such a staggering selection of varieties, you'll quickly discover that there is a perfect squash for whatever you want to cook.

Squash are native to North America but have been embraced by the global garden community, with varieties being developed in countries like China, Japan, and even Australia. There are three main species of winter squash: *Curcurbita pepo* (acorn, delicata, spaghetti), *C. moschata* (butternut, Musquée de Provence), and *C. maxima* (buttercup, banana, hubbard, kobocha).

Contrary to their name, winter squash are warm-season plants grown in summer. However, they are eaten in fall and winter, thanks to their hard, protective skin that forms a barrier against rot. A properly stored squash can last as long as 9 months in a cool basement or garage.

Winter squash come in a wide range of sizes, from modest, half-pound individual-sized fruits all the way up to monster-size squash that weigh over a hundred pounds. Popular types include acorn, butternut, buttercup, and delicata, but don't discount the many other wonderful kinds, including the Japanese types like kuri and kabocha.

TRY THIS!
Miniature Winter Squash

WINTER SQUASH VINES aren't shy about taking over your garden, often sprawling 10 to 15 feet in every direction. That doesn't mean they don't have a place in small gardens or even containers. Bush-type winter squashes take up less room, and they mature earlier, so they're good for shorter seasons, too.

'SWEET DUMPLING' (95 days). This is a great choice for gardeners who want single-serving fruits and shorter vines. For much of the growing season, the plants are compact, but they do stretch out as harvest nears. Each vine yields up to ten 4-inch-wide fruits that weigh less than a pound. The roundish-flat fruits are very pretty — creamy ivory with dark green stripes — and hide a bright orange interior. The fine-textured flesh is very sweet — even the kids love it!

'BUTTERSCOTCH' (100 days). This All-America Selections winner is simply outstanding. The tidy 3-foot vines are great for container gardens or small spaces, yet they yield a good crop of palm-size butternut squash. Too cute! The fruits weigh 1 to 2 pounds and have a very sweet flavor and smooth texture. Resistant to powdery mildew.

'BUSH DELICATA' (100 days). Another All-America Selections winner, 'Bush Delicata' is an easy-to-grow squash that won't take over your yard. The vines grow to about 4 feet and yield 1½- to 2-pound oval fruits with ivory skin and green stripes. The pale orange flesh is fine textured and sweet. The plants are resistant to powdery mildew.

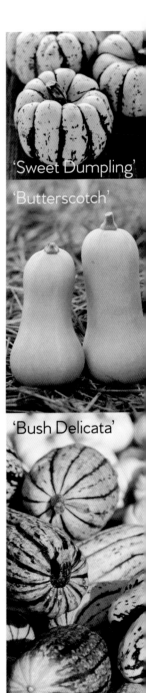

'Sweet Dumpling'

'Butterscotch'

'Bush Delicata'

TRY THIS!
Dense, Sweet Japanese Squash

WINTER SQUASH IS A POPULAR VEGETABLE in Asia, used in tempura, dumplings, soup, and stir-fry but also roasted or used in desserts. And although many North American types of winter squash grow large, sometimes up to 40 pounds per fruit, most Japanese types are smaller, with fruits weighing less than 5 pounds. Like more familiar varieties, Japanese winter squash are typically sweet with dense, smooth flesh.

KABOCHA TYPES (95 days). Similar in appearance and closely related to buttercup squash, kabocha varieties have a squat pumpkin shape, dry flesh, and an incredibly sweet flavor that is often compared to sweet potatoes. They can be deep green or bright orange or somewhere in between, but most will weigh in around 3 to 5 pounds. There are, however, miniature varieties like 'Shokichi Green' that produce tiny ½- to 1¼-pound squash. The fruits can be sliced and roasted, steamed, pureed into velvety soup, fried in tempura, stir-fried, or baked into pie. Other tasty varieties include 'Winter Sweet', 'Sunshine', and 'Hokkori'.

'RED KURI' (90–95 days). I can't say enough good things about 'Red Kuri'. First of all, at just 4 to 8 pounds, the fruits are the perfect size for a family meal or a modest amount of baking. They're also gorgeous: teardrop-shaped, with reddish orange skin and golden orange flesh. The flavor and texture? Think velvet — sweet, rich velvet. We use them in place of pumpkin in pies, breads, and muffins, but they're also delightful in soup or simply roasted in the oven. The vines are long and prolific; expect three to five fruits per vine.

'BLACK FUTSU' (105 days). 'Black Futsu' is a real looker; often unusually flattened, the fruits are dark green, almost black, but mature to a chestnut brown in storage. The interior flesh is deep orange and wonderful sliced for tempura, curry, or risotto. It's also great roasted with a bit of brown sugar or maple syrup. The bumpy, pebbly fruits will grow 3 to 5 pounds and range from softball to deflated-basketball size. The vines are very heavy producers, with anywhere from 4 to 10 fruits per plant.

'YOKOHAMA' (100 days). I have to confess that I originally grew this Japanese heirloom for its funny-looking fruits, with few expectations for its flavor. I figured that the squashed shape, deep ribs, and funny warts would appeal to the kids, who always seem interested in the weird and wonderful. They loved the odd shape, but we were also wowed by the sweet, almost fruity flavor and texture of the bright orange flesh. The fruits are compact, growing 6 to 7 inches across, with most in the 3- to 5-pound range.

'SHISHIGATANI' (110 days). This variety isn't going to win any beauty contests, but it's a quite a treat to eat! The odd-looking fruits are bottle-shaped and deep green in color, aging to a tannish brown. It has not only a rich flavor, but also a rich history. According to the Kitazawa Seed Company, "Since the Edo period of the early 1800s, this special Japanese pumpkin is one of the Kyo Yasai, or traditional vegetables in the Kyoto region. This kabocha squash is used in shojin ryori, a type of vegetarian cooking prepared by Buddhist priests." The yellow flesh is medium sweet and slightly stringy. Individual fruits range from 4 to 8 pounds, with two or three fruits per vine.

'Red Kuri'

'Kabocha'

'Kabocha'

'Black Futsu'

'Shishigatani'

'Lady Godiva'   'Musquée de Provence'

TRY THIS!

Other Weird and Wonderful Winter Squashes

MY FIRST INTRODUCTION TO the diverse range of winter squashes came during one of my Vegetable Crop Production labs when I was at university. The professor had laid out more than 30 varieties of baked winter squash in the classroom, and we had to sample each one. What a treat! So many sizes, colors, shapes, and textures and such a range of sweetness. Thus began my obsession with winter squash. Here are some of my favorite varieties, all unique heirlooms that are both prolific and easy to grow.

'LADY GODIVA' (105 days). Halloween might be my husband's favorite holiday, but not for the costumes or the candy; he loves the roasted pumpkin seeds! When it comes to delicious pumpkin seeds, it's hard to beat 'Lady Godiva'. It's also known as the naked seed pumpkin because its seeds

are hull-less — perfect for roasting. You can eat the pumpkin flesh, too, but we find it a bit bland. The fruits themselves have attractive orange-green rinds and weigh 4 to 6 pounds.

'JUMBO PINK BANANA' (100 days). This novel squash boasts an eye-popping color combination of pale salmon-pink skin with a bright gold interior flesh. The fruit really does resemble a giant pink banana, and under ideal conditions, they can reach lengths of 30 inches and weigh up to 40 pounds. That's a lot of squash! The flesh is firm and dry, sweet with a mild nutty flavor. This is also an excellent keeper; the squash will last months in cool storage. Expect three or four fruits per vine.

'MUSQUÉE DE PROVENCE' (120 days). I always feel a bit guilty cutting up this French heirloom; it's just so beautiful! The fruits have a flattened, deeply ribbed shape and mature from dark green to a lovely tan color. My guilt doesn't last long, though. We adore the taste of it! The thick, deep orange, richly flavored flesh is sweet, but not *too* sweet. 'Musquée de Provence' (sometimes called 'Musquée d'Hiver de

Provence') is a long-season variety, but well worth trying even for gardeners with shorter growing seasons. The fruits are usually between 12 and 15 pounds, though I have gotten a few that weighed well over 30 pounds! The long vines can yield three to five fruits each, and the plants are more resistant to powdery mildew than other varieties. Properly cured, the squash will last at least 6 months in storage.

'GALEUX D'EYSINES' (105 days). I was introduced to this French heirloom by a neighbor who saw a catalog picture of the strange cheese-wheel-shape squash, covered in peanuty warts, and "had to have it." I didn't have room for any more squash that season, and so I watched this variety grow in her garden. The long vines each yielded two or three big fruits, weighing 10 to 15 pounds apiece. As summer yielded to autumn, it became obvious the seed catalog hadn't exaggerated. We were all enchanted! And we thought the silky-smooth, bright gold flesh made the best squash soup.

'LAKOTA' (90–100 days). A variety that originated with the Lakota Sioux, 'Lakota' yields incredibly decorative pear-shaped fruits with orange-red skin and bold green stripes. The kids love it! Expect long vines, running 15 or more feet, with three or four basketball-size fruits per plant. The flavor is sweet and sublime, with a dry texture. 'Lakota' is also a good keeper.

'MARINA DI CHIOGGIA' (100 days). I first came upon this rare Italian heirloom at our local farmers' market, where a small pile of the lumpy, warted fruits were sitting at the front of a farm stand. They were big (about 10 to 15 pounds each), squat, and emerald green in color. I was originally seduced by their bubbly appearance but totally won over by their rich, dense texture and sweet, sweet flavor.

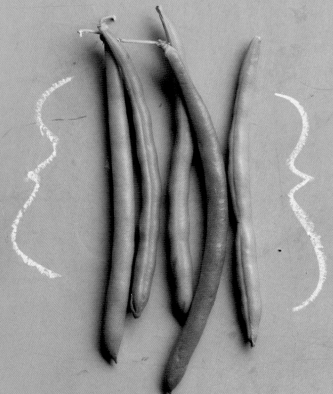

like snap beans?

Hyacinth beans

try these!

Edamame

Chickpeas

Yard-long beans

If it weren't for the simple snap bean, I would probably not be writing this book. It was my childhood love of yellow wax beans that prompted me to try my hand at growing vegetables. Even today, home-grown beans remain one of my favorite garden crops.

Because I'm a bean fanatic, I also appreciate the spectacular snap bean stands-ins. How about noodle beans, which can grow several feet in length? Or the unusual deep purple pods of hyacinth beans, which look *and* taste incredible? Or chickpeas, which we gobble up fresh from the garden? While you're at it, why not give daylily buds a try? Yup, you read that right: *daylily buds.* Read on, my friend.

TRY THIS!
Yard-long Beans

THESE FELLOW MEMBERS of the legume family don't taste exactly like snap beans, but rather have a flavor that is all their own. Author and heirloom vegetable expert Marie Iannotti describes the distinctive taste of 'Red Noodle' yard-long beans as "a whisper of legume flavor, with layers of the earthier flavors of asparagus, mushrooms, and their cowpea cousins." I couldn't agree more!

In addition to producing uniquely flavored pods, the plants are super ornamental: bright green foliage and pretty blooms are followed by the long ribbons of beans. The beans can grow to be more than 2 feet long, though for optimum flavor and texture, most varieties should be picked when they're just 12 to 15 inches long.

It almost goes without saying that if you have young children, yard-longs are a must. Once the pods form, our kids love to measure their growth every day. And when they're ready to eat, you might find that you don't have to convince your kids to eat their veggies; they'll be happy to gobble these up. You could steam or boil them, as you would snap beans, but I've found that their flavor really stands out when they're stir-fried or sautéed.

THE DETAILS

A.K.A.: Asparagus beans, noodle beans, snake beans, Chinese long beans, *Vigna unguiculata* subsp. *sesquipedalis*

DAYS TO MATURITY: 80–85 days

HAILS FROM: Southern Asia

VARIETIES TO TRY: 'Liana', 'Red Noodle', 'Orient Wonder'

'Red Noodle'

YARD-LONG BEANS YOU SHOULD GROW

'LIANA' (70–75 days). One of the earliest maturing and most reliable varieties, 'Liana' can set pods just 2 months from seeding (truthfully, though, in my garden it's closer to 2½ months). The slender pods are deep green and borne in clusters, beginning in midsummer. Pick often to encourage a heavy harvest.

'RED NOODLE' (80 days). Among the most beautiful of the yard-long beans, 'Red Noodle' has pretty lavender blooms, followed by long, dark red pods that stand out dramatically against bright green leaves. When stir-fried or sautéed, the beans retain their deep color, but if boiled, expect some of that color to bleed out. I've had success with them during warm summers, especially when I start the seeds indoors and prewarm the garden soil before planting out.

nice nectaries!

One of the coolest things about yard-long beans is that they have extrafloral nectaries on the stems that produce their flowers. These are glands that secrete nectar, not for the purpose of attracting pollinators, but rather to entice beneficial insects. In the case of yard-long beans, they are attracting insects like wasps and ants, which will defend the plants from many common pests. So leave the ants and wasps to their business. If you see aphids on the plants, though, knock them off with a jet of water from your hose or spray with a soap solution.

'ORIENT WONDER' (70 days). This popular variety is tolerant of both hot and cool temperatures. It bears a heavy crop of dark green pods, but the interior seeds are slow to mature, meaning the pods maintain their eating quality for a long time.

GIVE THEM A HEAD START

The first year I grew yard-long beans, I direct-seeded the variety 'Red Noodle' in late May at the same time I sowed my pole beans. Germination was sporadic, growth was very slow, and the plants produced only a few modest-size beans. I was not impressed.

The next year, I gave 'Red Noodle' a second chance, but I also tried 'Liana', an earlier-maturing variety. I soaked the seeds overnight and started the seeds indoors a few weeks before transplanting. I planted the seeds in 4-inch pots and placed the pots on top of my fridge for bottom heat. Germination happened in about a week, and I tucked the young seedlings into the garden 10 days later.

Since my failure the previous year, I had done some research and learned that yard-long beans don't like cold soil. So I covered the garden bed with black plastic for 2 weeks to warm the soil before I planted the seedlings (about a week after our average last frost date). The result was dramatic — all but one of the seedlings took (and that one was a casualty of slug damage).

A BIT OF COMPOST, A LOT OF SUPPORT

Yard-long beans have fairly basic needs. Like many vegetables, they should be planted where they'll receive at least 6 hours of direct sunlight a day. Dig in some compost, but don't go overboard; the plants aren't greedy feeders. One secret to the best-tasting yard-long beans, though, is regular moisture. Irrigate weekly and mulch the soil to conserve water.

If you're direct seeding, wait until all risk of frost has passed and space the seeds every 3 inches, eventually thinning plants to 6 inches apart. If you're transplanting, plant hardened-off seedlings every 6 inches. Provide vertical supports or a fence for the vines, which will grow 8 to 12 feet long. There are a few varieties that grow in bush form, but most yard-long beans are vigorous vines that need a strong support. Certain varieties, like 'Red Noodle', are reluctant climbers, but with a little early coaching, you can encourage the vines to twine around their supports.

EAT SHOOTS AND LEAVES

The main crop of yard-longs will be the slender bean pods, but the shoot tips and young leaves are also edible and can be lightly stir-fry or sautéed. If you grow more than one variety, you may note subtle flavor differences in the pods. The varieties with lighter green pods are sweeter and milder, while the dark green pods have a deeper taste. The red varieties are even more complex, with tones of bean mixed with a mild nuttiness and hints of mushroom. If you expect a snap bean flavor, you may be disappointed. Instead, I'd suggest you seek out Asian-inspired recipes to take advantage of this wonderful vegetable.

Pick often to encourage the longest harvest. Look for pods that are around pencil diameter, or slightly smaller, but at least 10 to 15 inches long. They should also be smooth, not bumpy — which would indicate that the interior seeds are maturing. Once they pass peak quality, I find the pods can get a unpleasant, spongy texture, similar to that of overmature snap beans.

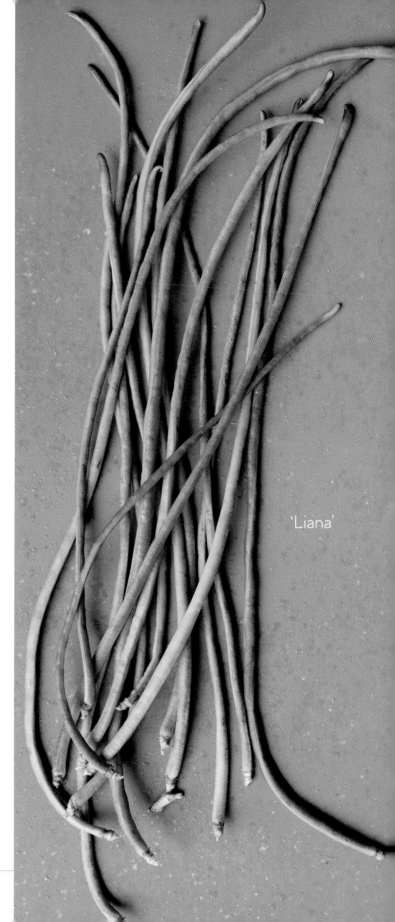

'Liana'

TRY THIS!
Hyacinth Beans

THE DETAILS

A.K.A.: Lablab, Egyptian bean, bonavista bean, *Lablab purpureus*

DAYS TO MATURITY: 90–100 days

HAILS FROM: South Asia

VARIETIES TO TRY: 'Moonshadow', 'Ruby Moon', 'Purple Moon'

HYACINTH BEANS KNOW HOW to throw a garden party! The vining plants are incredibly ornamental with purple-tinged leaves and stems and showy clusters of violet-purple flowers. But the true stars of the show are the shiny purple seedpods that are produced from midsummer until frost. Of course, not all hyacinth beans have purple flowers and pods; there are some white-flowering varieties with green pods. But for a punch of color, you can't beat the purple varieties.

In North America, hyacinth beans are primarily grown as an annual ornamental vine; the lilac-purple clusters of blooms also make excellent cut flowers. In many Asian and African countries, though, it's a common food crop. The plants offer multiple harvests: the leaves, flowers, and immature pods are all edible. In India, the young pods — which have a strong bean flavor with earthy tones — are often stir-fried or added to curry. The mature seeds are also edible, but they contain a toxic compound and must be thoroughly cooked before they are eaten.

HYACINTH LIKES IT HOT

Given their tropical origins, it makes sense that hyacinth beans need heat to thrive; the white-flowering types demand an even longer season than the purple varieties (another reason to grow purple). If you live in a climate with a short growing season, you'll want to start the seeds indoors a few weeks before the last expected frost (see page 62). In the garden, give them a sunny spot that is sheltered from wind and offers decent, amended soil. The vines may grow from 8 to 15 feet, depending on your location, so provide something strong for them to climb.

These are gorgeous plants — make sure you pick a spot where you can enjoy the show! Few insects or diseases bother them, though I have had one occurrence of powdery mildew on my vines. I've also found the best-quality pods are produced when the plants are given ample water; be sure to mulch plants well and irrigate regularly.

EAT THEM YOUNG

The first harvest from hyacinth beans comes from the young foliage, which can be picked and cooked like spinach. This is soon followed by the lilac-purple blooms, which have a mild bean flavor and can be tossed raw into salads or used to garnish sweet and savory dishes. Pick pods while they're still immature — around 1½ inches long and still tender — and use them as a substitute for snow peas in recipes. De-string them and stir-fry, sauté, or steam. Once the seeds inside the pods begin to mature and change color, toxic cyanogenic glucosides build up. At this point, the beans and seeds need to be well cooked before eating, a process that breaks up the toxic compounds.

TRY THIS!
Buttery Edamame Beans

WANT TO KNOW WHAT disappears quicker than a bowl of chips? A bowl of freshly picked, steamed, and salted edamame! As soon as I place them on the table, everyone grabs a handful of pods to slurp out the nutty, buttery beans hidden within. These are actually young, tender soybeans, though they're a far cry from their field crop brethren.

EDAMAME YOU SHOULD GROW

'ENVY' (75–80 days). I've tried several cultivars over the years, but we always come back to 'Envy', a reliable short-season soybean that has become a standard for northern gardeners. Plants will grow about 2 feet tall and yield a good crop of bright green pods, each pod containing two or three tender beans.

'MIDORI GIANT' (80–90 days). Dependable, high yielding, and low maintenance, 'Midori Giant' is a popular pick for home gardeners. The early-maturing, compact plants grow just under 2 feet tall but are heavily branched and loaded with pods. Almost all of the pods will have two or three large buttery beans inside.

'SHIROFUMI' (90–95 days). Another winner for cool climates, 'Shirofumi' is extremely productive. Most of the pods will contain two or three seeds, but they're very large seeds that fill their plump pods. Like most edamame varieties, the harvest season is short, so plant in succession for a prolonged harvest.

WARM IT UP

Soybeans are not difficult to grow, but they do resent cold soil; the seeds will either sulk or rot, and germination rates will nosedive. Be patient and wait until the soil has warmed up to at least 65°F (18°C) before planting. If you just can't stand the wait, you can prewarm the soil by covering it with a sheet of black plastic for 2 weeks prior to seeding.

Direct sow the seeds about 2 inches apart in a compost-enriched bed that receives full sun; germination will take 10 to 14 days. Thin seedlings to 4 to 6 inches apart once they're growing well. For an extended harvest, stagger your plantings, sowing fresh seed every 10 to 14 days.

Plants will grow to be bushy and compact, between 1 and 3 feet tall. Keep them evenly moist, giving them about an inch of water per week if there has been no rain. Mulching plants with shredded leaves or straw will help maintain soil moisture. Deer and rabbits seem to be the main pests.

HARVEST DAILY

Harvest pods when they're plump and bright green. They will mature within a relatively short period of 10 to 14 days, so check for ready-to-pick pods every day or so. If you wait too long to harvest, the beans inside the pods will turn from sweet to starchy. You know they're approaching overmaturity when the pods begin to turn yellow.

THE DETAILS

A.K.A.: Soybean, *Glycine max*

DAYS TO MATURITY: 60 days for fresh, 85–90 days for dried

HAILS FROM: China

VARIETIES TO TRY: 'Envy', 'Midori Giant', 'Shirofumi'

TRY THIS!
Fresh Chickpeas

EVERY SPRING my father-in-law cultivates a modest 10- by 10-foot plot in his sunny backyard. The soil isn't great (rocky, weedy, and clay based), but he loosens it and scatters chickpea seeds on the surface, raking to bury the seeds. He gives no thought to pre-starting the seeds, enriching the soil, spacing the rows, or fertilizing. He doesn't even buy seed packets or look for special varieties; he simply opens a package of dried chickpeas, sold for cooking, and grabs a handful. And yet, every August, his crop is reliable, yielding a good harvest of small green pods with one to three chickpeas tucked inside. Go figure!

Although our family eats chickpeas or chickpea-based dishes like hummus on an almost daily basis, all of our homegrown chickpeas are consumed fresh like *petit pois*, shelled and eaten immediately. Of course, you can grow chickpeas to dry and store for winter dishes, but the plants are not super productive, and you would need a lot of space for a good-size harvest.

CHICKPEAS YOU SHOULD TRY

KABULI and **DESI TYPES.** Although it's hard to find named varieties of chickpeas in catalogs, you can choose from the two main groups: large-seeded "kabuli" and smaller-seeded "desi." Kabuli types make up the majority of chickpeas grown in North America, and desi types are popular in the Middle East and India. 'Kabuli' and 'Desi' are sometimes listed as cultivars in seed catalogs.

'BLACK KABULI' (80 days fresh, 100 days dried), also seen as 'Kabouli Black'. This unusual variety is available from Baker Creek as well as Salt Spring Seeds (distribution in Canada only). When mature, it has purple-black seeds. It is well adapted to my cool climate, reliably growing well and ready to pick as a "green crop" in mid-August.

'CHICKPEA OF SPELLO' (80–85 days fresh, 100 days dried). An Italian variety, this one is lovely when eaten as a fresh shell bean. The plants grow up to 2 feet and produce a high number of the small, bright green pods.

EASY CHICKPEASY . . .
Like my father-in-law, I also find chickpeas easy to grow. I do put a little more care into crop selection and planting preparation, though, which pays off with an earlier and larger harvest. I plant chickpeas in a sunny

bed with well-drained average soil. The "well-drained" part is very important, as chickpeas will quickly die if left with wet feet. Chickpeas also won't yield well in rich soil — a lesson I learned when I babied my first crop, amending with plenty of aged manure and organic fertilizers before planting. By midsummer, I had beautiful lush plants, but only a handful of pods. Oops! Now I just amend the soil with an inch or so of compost before planting.

. . . IF PLANTED AT THE RIGHT TIME

Chickpeas are a long-season vegetable and grow best in regions with long periods of cool to warm temperatures. The planting date for chickpeas can determine the success of your crop, especially for those in regions with short growing seasons. Plant too early and the seeds will rot in the cold spring soil; plant too late and yields may decline because the plants are exposed to temperatures above 85°F (29°C) during flowering. Extended high temperatures can cause buds, flowers, or pods to drop.

So, when to plant? Direct seed around a month before the last expected spring frost. Plant the seed about 1½ inches deep and 3 inches apart, eventually thinning to 6 inches apart. I've also had success starting the seeds indoors 4 to 5 weeks before the expected last frost date and moving the young seedlings to the garden once the danger of frost has passed. Germination will take 7 to 10 days, depending on soil temperature and moisture.

PRETTY AND NOT FUSSY AT ALL

Chickpea plants will grow up to 2 feet tall and form a dense mat of lacy, gray-green foliage with small, pealike flowers in shades of white, purple, or pink emerging in midsummer. As such, they make a very pretty edge along a perennial garden. They're also pretty in containers, but don't expect them to produce a large harvest when planted that way. I do give the bed an inch of water per week if there has been no rain, but the plants are quite drought tolerant and need little fussing.

If you've never grown this crop before, it is helpful to order a packet of the inoculant, as it will certainly boost yield. The bacterium is a different strain than what is commonly used for snap beans, so be sure to order chickpea-specific inoculant.

THE DETAILS

A.K.A.: Garbanzo beans, *Cicer arietinum*

DAYS TO MATURITY: 80 days for fresh, 100 days for dried

HAILS FROM: Middle East

VARIETIES TO TRY: 'Black Kabuli', 'Chickpea of Spello'

GOOD GREEN PODS

We prefer to harvest our crop when the pods are immature; at this stage, the wrinkly, green seeds inside have a delicious pea-bean flavor. Sometimes we turn excess young seeds into a fresh hummus, but more often than not we all gather at the table with a pile of the pulled plants, grabbing the pods and squeezing out the seeds to eat raw like shell peas. It's an annual family tradition that we all look forward to. Excess green chickpeas can also be blanched and frozen for a winter dish of green hummus.

For dried beans, allow the pods to dry on the plants, and then shell and gather the dried seeds. If damp weather threatens the crop, pull the almost-dry plants and hang them in an airy place indoors to finish the drying process.

wanted: hunan winged bean

This curious plant, also called the Asian winged bean (*Psophocarpus tetragonolobus*), four-angled bean, dragon bean, and winged pea, is on my "to-grow" list. Acclaimed plant historian William Woys Weaver says the winged bean is an attractive climbing vine with many edible parts: the long, green pods, the seeds, young shoots, the deep green leaves, the small purple flowers, and the tubers. The pods, which should be picked when 3 inches long or less, are popular in Asian markets and gardens and have a flavor similar to that of green beans. The plants are tropical in origin and need full sun and well-drained soil. Northern gardeners should start the seeds indoors, moving the seedlings to the garden once the risk of frost has passed and the weather has warmed.

TRY THIS!
Delicious Daylily

ANYONE WHO HAS GROWN DAYLILIES knows just how low maintenance and care-free these popular perennials are. They'll grow in full sun as well as partial shade, and they are drought, pest, disease and even (relatively) deer resistant. Their common name comes from their blooming habit, with each flower lasting just a day. But they could just as easily be called "green-bean lilies," because that's what the buds taste like. In fact, most parts of the daylily plant are edible: early spring shoots, flower buds, open blooms, young leaves, and even the tubers. (See page 69 for more details on the tubers.)

In their native Asia, daylilies are appreciated as both a food crop and an ornamental plant. In our garden, we affectionately call the flower buds "daylily beans" for their appearance and flavor, which is similar to fresh green beans, with hints of asparagus. The taste is quite sweet, and we typically give them a quick stir-fry for an unbeatable side dish.

This is a fun crop for foraging fans, who can hunt out the orange "ditch lilies" that have gone wild in many parts of North America. But you can also forage for daylilies in your own yard. Just make sure you get your lilies right. Daylilies are edible, but *true* lilies — those in the genus *Lilium*, like Oriental or Asiatic lilies — are not edible. If you're unsure what type of lilies you have in your yard, ask a local expert.

GROWING DAYLILIES

Ellen Zachos, author and foraging expert, suggests sticking to the straight species, *Hemerocallis fulva*. She acknowledges that there are thousands of cultivars, but she can only vouch for the safety of the familiar, orange-flowered species.

For the best bud crop, plant your daylilies in full sun, with at least 6 hours of direct light. They will grow in partial shade, but they will produce far fewer buds. I've planted most of my daylilies in perennial gardens, but I also have a patch tucked within the confines of the deer fence that surrounds our vegetable garden. They add a blast of summer color, provide weeks of tender "daylily beans," and attract pollinators and other beneficial insects to the crops.

GATHER YE BUDS

Unopened flower buds can be harvested when they're just a scant inch long and up until they're about 3 inches long and starting to reveal a hint of color. Zachos recommends a quick cooking to let the flavor of the buds shine. "My favorite way to eat the flower buds is a simple sauté with olive oil and a touch of garlic," she says. You can also impress dinner guests by dipping the raw buds into a beer tempura batter and deep-frying until golden.

You can also add daylily petals to salads for a pop of color: tear them into smaller pieces and sprinkle on top of your favorite combination of mixed greens. The whole flowers can be stuffed like squash blossoms and pan-fried until they're crispy. Or crystalize the blossoms with sugar to adorn cakes and dessert trays.

Daylilies offer many edible parts, but my favorites are the flower buds, which we call "daylily beans," and the tender tubers that look like tiny fingerling potatoes (page 182).

Keep in mind that people with food allergies or sensitive stomachs should proceed with caution and try just a small quantity of daylily buds to start. Allergic reactions are rare but not unheard of. For certain people, the buds can also have a mild laxative effect. Your dinner guests may not be impressed by that.

THE DETAILS

A.K.A.: Ditch lily, *Hemerocallis fulva*

DAYS TO MATURITY: Perennial plant in Zones 3 to 9

HAILS FROM: Eastern Asia

VARIETIES TO TRY: Any variety of *H. fulva* will be edible.

WHY GROW ORDINARY SNAP BEANS?

'Dragon's Tongue'

'Red Swan'

'French Gold'

'Emerite'

EACH SUMMER, WE GROW a rainbow of beans: purple, green, yellow, red, and even some, like 'Dragon's Tongue', that have distinctive bicolored pods. Early on, I planted mostly bush varieties, which are easy to grow, quick to crop, and don't need staking or a structure to climb. Soon, however, I discovered pole beans. At the beginning of the season, it's a bit more work to erect their structures, and they do start yielding their pods a week or two after bush beans, but that harvest goes on for a very long time — months, not weeks — and the overall production per plant is at least twice that of bush beans. Plus, the vines are super ornamental and attractive to pollinators like hummingbirds.

'BLAUHILDE' (65 days). This delightful German heirloom is both beautiful and super productive, yielding 8- to 10-foot vines with pretty lavender-purple flowers followed by dark purple pods. The beans can grow up to 10 inches long, but expect the best-quality pods to be in the 6- to 8-inch range.

'DRAGON'S TONGUE' (60 days). If you prefer bush beans to pole beans, give 'Dragon's Tongue' a try. The compact plants are relatively quick to bear their crop of distinctive greenish yellow pods that are streaked in bright purple. Unfortunately, they do lose the purple color when cooked.

'RED SWAN' (54 days). This bush bean was bred by renowned bean breeder Robert Lobitz and is the result of crossing a pinto bean with a purple snap bean. The attractive flowers are white with pink, and are quickly followed by 4- to 6-inch-long burgundy-pink, flat pods.

'NEW MEXICO CAVE BEAN' (60 days snap, 90 days dried). History buffs will love

'Blauhilde'

growing this ancient variety, which is said to have been found in a sealed clay pot in a cave in New Mexico. It's also called 'Aztec Cave' or Anasazi bean and yields 8-foot-tall vines that bear a heavy crop of 6- to 7-inch-long flat snap beans. If eaten as a snap, they do need to be stringed. The seeds from mature pods can be saved and used as dried beans.

'GOLD MARIE' (70–75 days). Our crop of yellow beans is one of the highlights of my summer, and when I read about 'Gold Marie', an heirloom pole variety, I was eager to try it in my garden. It was a happy discovery, as the vines grew quickly and easily, scaling a bamboo tepee and wandering over to a nearby

A-frame trellis. The butter-yellow pods were flat and grew huge — up to 10 inches long, though we tried to pick them in the 6- to 7-inch range. Definitely a keeper.

'TONELLO' (70 days). According to my friends at Annapolis Seeds, "This pole bean was brought to Canada from Italy by Santo Luigi Tonello. He and his wife, Yolanda, settled in Liverpool, Nova Scotia, in 1921, and on a return trip to Italy, they brought back a small handful of these beans hidden in his shirt pocket." The vigorous vines bear a heavy harvest of flat green pods, maturing to soft yellow, that can be eaten as a snap or allowed to mature for dried beans.

'Golden Sunshine'

'JIMENEZ' (80 days). A few years ago, a friend who visited Spain brought back a packet of these heirloom beans for me. They were like no bean I had ever grown before. The pods were thick and meaty, flat and broad, and deep green in color, but heavily streaked in carmine red. Absolutely gorgeous! Of course, the color does fade when the beans are cooked, but the rich flavor and vigorous production of this pole bean make it worth growing.

'GOLDEN SUNSHINE' (80 days). Not a snap bean but a type of runner bean, which, unlike pole beans, are well known for their ability to crop reliably in cool, wet climates. This beauty is worth growing for its stunning lime green foliage and bright red flowers that are a hummingbird favorite. The beans are just a bonus! The rampant vines, which are more tolerant of cool weather than pole beans, will grow up to 10 feet long and yield an abundant harvest of green beans. These are best harvested at 4 to 6 inches long, but we also let some of the beans mature for dried beans; shelling the large, beautiful beans from their papery pods is a fun task for the kids.

'TONGUES OF FIRE' (65 days). These heirloom beans came to me from Ushuaia, Argentina, the southernmost city in the world, where they are said to originate. They're also popular in Italy, where they are called 'Borlotto' and eaten as fresh snaps or matured and dried for their pretty white-and-pink speckled seeds. When they first emerge, the pods are pale green with fiery red streaks; the green deepens as the pods mature, and the red color remains.

'Gold Marie'

'Gold Marie'

'Tongues of Fire'

like peas?

try these
unusual varieties!

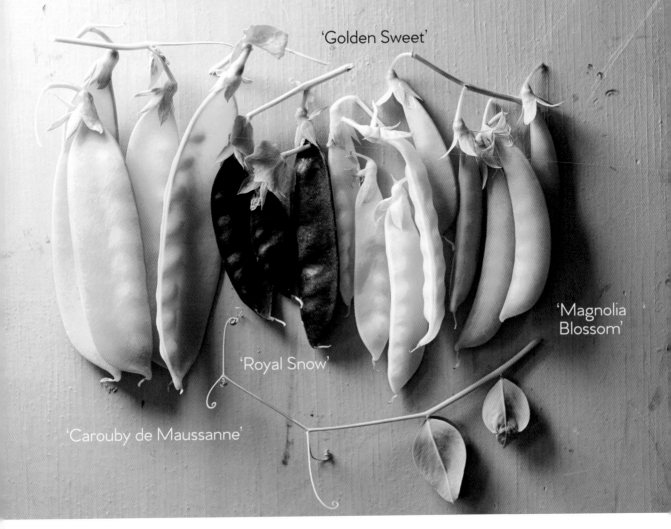

'Golden Sweet'

'Magnolia Blossom'

'Royal Snow'

'Carouby de Maussanne'

In our garden, 'Sugar Snap' is the pea of choice, but that doesn't stop us from experimenting with other varieties, especially those with unique colors like 'King Tut' or 'Opal Creek'. We also like peas that produce extra-large pods, like 'Carouby de Maussane', or those that have tiny peas, like the *petit pois* variety 'Iona'.

Some of the unique peas listed below are recent introductions, bred by respected and well-known breeders like Dr. Alan Kapuler of Peace Seeds, who has spent decades fostering plant biodiversity. Others are treasured heirlooms, appreciated by gardeners for centuries. Whichever varieties you choose to grow, I hope you enjoy the exceptional quality and flavor of these unusual peas.

'Magnolia Blossom'

'KING TUT' (70 days fresh, 100 days dried). The tale behind this striking pea is that it was found in the tomb of King Tut. I'm a little skeptical about the story, but I'm convinced that this is a variety every pea-loving gardener should try. The plants grow to a modest 3 feet in height, but when the electric blue blooms open, this will be the most beautiful plant in your garden. As the flowers fade, eye-catching deep purple

'Blue Pod Capucijner'

pods emerge that can be picked young as a sugar pea or allowed to fatten up for shell peas. Overmature pods can be left to dry on the plant for soup.

'BLUE POD CAPUCIJNER' (70 days fresh, 100 days dried). Purple-blue on the outside, green on the inside, these shelling peas are a big hit with all the kids who visit our garden! Their history is entwined with the Franciscan Capuchin monks in Europe, who grew them in the sixteenth century. Today, we appreciate their bicolored flowers (pink and red), unusual maroon-purple pods that mature to a brownish blue, and the productive plants that grow 5 feet tall.

'CAROUBY DE MAUSSANE' (65 days). Who says size doesn't matter? Certainly not

'Tom Thumb'   'Sugar Magnolia'

'Carouby de Maussane', an heirloom snow pea with pods that grow up to 6 inches in length! There is a lot to love about this variety; the vigorous 5- to 6-foot-tall plants, the two-toned maroon-and-pink flowers, and the massive 5- to 6-inch flat pods that maintain their tenderness, even when grown to gargantuan size. We love to stir-fry the pods when they're at peak quality, 3 to 4 inches long, but we also use them in hodgepodge, a Nova Scotian vegetable chowder, which is my favorite summer treat!

'IONA' (68 days). Good things come in small packages, and 'Iona' is the perfect example of this. Considered a *petit pois* shell pea, its compact 2- to 2½-foot-tall vines will yield a generous crop of 3-inch-long pods filled with minuscule peas; only about half the size of normal peas. Yes, these are more time consuming to pick and shell. But miniature peas with a delicious sweet flavor? Yes, it's worth it.

'OPAL CREEK' (60 days). This curious pea was bred by Dr. Alan Kapuler of Peace Seeds and has butter-yellow pods. These should be picked while still tender and flat, like a snow pea, and can be stir-fried, steamed, or added to salads.

'TOM THUMB' (55 days). I was first introduced to 'Tom Thumb' when I was looking for compact cold-season crops for our cold frames. Given its diminutive size — just 8 inches — 'Tom Thumb' seemed like a perfect fit! We now sow them in our frames

'Magnolia Blossom'

in late summer, as well as in early spring for a soil-building crop of sweet shelling peas. Each pod yields about five or six tender peas. This is also a fabulous container crop and can be direct sown in pots or window boxes.

'SUGAR MAGNOLIA' (70 days). This remarkable pea, also developed by Dr. Kapuler, is the first purple-podded sugar snap. The plants will grow 6 to 7 feet tall and offer ornamental interest when the bright purple flowers open. Soon, the vivid purple pods appear; the kids love to gobble them up while standing in the pea patch.

The best flavor comes from the pods just as they start to fatten.

'MAGNOLIA BLOSSOM' (80 days). Another Dr. Kapuler introduction, 'Magnolia Blossom' is a beautiful, productive pea with sweet flavor and unusual coloring. Give the vines a sturdy support, as they will reach 7 to 8 feet. The snap pods will be green, with some having a distinctive purple stripe down the side when mature. For peak quality, they should really be picked before the stripe appears, but those funky stripes are very appealing! The vines also produce edible hypertendrils that can be picked to add

'Golden Sweet'

'Petite Snap-Greens'

a green pea flavor to salads and stir-fries or used as an unusual garnish.

'GOLDEN SWEET' (65 days). I can't vouch for its history, but I've read that this showy snow pea was discovered in a market in India, eventually making its way to heirloom-seed catalogs across North America and Europe. Whatever its backstory, it's definitely garden gold, producing tall, productive vines with purple flowers and bright yellow pods.

'PETITE SNAP-GREENS' (30 days). Unlike most peas, which are bred for tender, delicious pods, this quirky variety has been developed for its edible tendrils, leaves,

and stems! Dr. Calvin Lamborn is the breeder — the pea genius who introduced 'Sugar Snap' and has won multiple All-America Selections awards for his cultivars. 'Petite Snap-Greens' offers modest vines that grow to about 3 feet tall, but you should harvest them when they're still small — 6 to 8 inches tall — by cutting them above the first node. This will encourage subsequent harvests of the tender pea shoots. These can also be seeded in cold frames in late winter for an early spring crop or in late summer for a fall crop. Add the tasty tendrils to salads or toss them in pasta.

like eggplants?

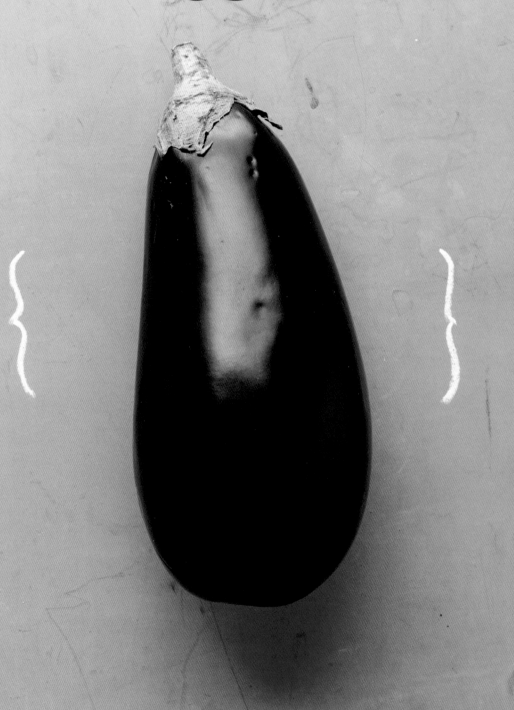

try these unusual varieties!

FOR SUCH AN EXOTIC-LOOKING CROP, eggplants — even the quirky ones! — are surprisingly easy to grow. And with such diversity in fruit shape, size, and color, why not try some "novelty" eggplants, which include milky white varieties like 'Casper' (the friendly eggplant!) or 'Turkish Orange', a popular heirloom with rounded orange fruits?

'CASPER' (75 days) has a number of outstanding characteristics. First, it's absolutely gorgeous, with milky white, teardrop-shaped fruits. It's also more tolerant of cooler summers, making it a good choice for gardeners in Zones 4 to 6. The plants are productive and yield a good crop of the 5- to 6-inch-long eggplants. The flavor and texture are often compared to the meatiness of mushrooms, but to me it's more subtle and quite creamy, especially when roasted or grilled.

'TURKISH ORANGE' (80 days) is an intriguing African heirloom that looks more like a small pumpkin than an eggplant. When ripe, fruits are bright orange with greenish streaks and bright green calyxes and stems. They grow just 3 inches in diameter on compact, prickly plants. The fruits look most ornamental when fully ripe, but they reach their culinary peak when they're still immature: green or just beginning to blush orange. If you wait until they're deep orange, they'll be seedy and bitter. We like to roast ¼-inch-thick slices of the green fruits until soft and add them to salads or bread and fry them for a tasty treat.

'Casper'

'LISTADA DE GANDIA' (85–90 days). A long-season eggplant, this variety needs plenty of heat to ripen and produce its fruits. But what fruits! They grow 4 to 6 inches long and are a stunning white streaked in lavender purple. Gardeners in Zones 5 and 6 should preheat their soil and use a mini hoop tunnel for the first month. Then, keep your fingers crossed for a hot summer!

'ROSA BIANCA' (80 days). Among the most popular garden varieties, this Italian heirloom has plump, rounded, white-and-violet fruits that grow to the size of a softball. Their flesh is mild and incredibly tender, and we like to roast them or stuff them with meat, rice, and spices. Expect the fruits to grow 5 to 6 inches across and have thin skin and no trace of bitterness.

'Turkish Orange'

'Listada de Gandia'

'Italian White'

'Bride'

'Ping Tung'

'Millionaire'

'Gretel'

'Casper'

'Thai long green'

Nonbitter Asian Eggplants

MY FAVORITE EGGPLANTS are the Asian varieties. They offer gourmet-quality fruits that are often long and slender, with very thin skin (no peeling required), few seeds, and nonbitter flesh. Plus, they're perfect for garden beds or containers, growing 18 to 24 inches tall and bearing a heavy crop of tender fruits from mid to late summer.

'MILLIONAIRE' (65 days). Expect this early-maturing Japanese hybrid to be one of the first to fruit in your garden. It's a proven performer, yielding a heavy crop of slender, deep purple, 8- to 10-inch fruits.

'MA-ZU' (75 days). Widely grown in its native Taiwan, the vigorous plants of 'Ma-Zu' produce a good crop of slender deep purple fruits, 10 to 12 inches long, but just 1½ to 2 inches across. The plants grow heavy with the fruit and should be supported or caged. Typical of Asian eggplants, the attractive fruits of this variety are thin skinned, tender, and almost seedless.

'ICHIBAN' (60 days). Reliable, productive, and delicious, 'Ichiban' is a popular Japanese eggplant that produces 8- to 10-inch-long, narrow, dark purple fruits with thin skin and creamy, sweet flesh. I like 'Ichiban' because it seems to tolerate a cool summer better than many other varieties, and it has ornamental foliage: deep green with purple veins.

'PING TUNG' (70 days). Eggplant varieties can be hit or miss in my northern garden. This one is definitely a hit! It originates from P'ing-tung in Taiwan and produces gorgeous slim lavender-purple fruits that grow 12 to 14 inches long and 1½ inches across. You can also pick them as baby eggplants, harvesting when the fruits are just 4 to 5 inches long. They are nonbitter, with thin skin and few seeds. Expect the bushy plants to yield 15 to 20 fruits per plant.

'KURUME LONG' (65 days). This open-pollinated Japanese favorite is early to mature and yields purple-black fruits with thin glossy skin. They will grow about 6 to 8 inches long and be 1½ to 2 inches wide. Great for frying, stir-frying, tempura, roasting, and pickling.

'BRIDE' (75 days). The first time I grew this one, I didn't want to pick the fruits because they were just so beautiful; creamy white streaked in lavender. They'll grow 6 to 8 inches long and be just over 1 inch in diameter when mature. The mild flesh is white with few seeds. The lavender-pink flowers are also highly decorative. This is a great variety to grow in a big pot on a sunny deck or patio where the flowers and fruits can be admired.

'THAI LONG GREEN' (85 days). These fruits are almost too pretty to eat! Chartreuse green in color, they're also slim and can grow more than 1 foot long but are only 1½ inches wide. They have outstanding flavor, thin skin, and firm white flesh.

success in containers

Eggplants take well to container growing; my potted crops sometimes out-produce my garden plants! This is because my back deck is very sunny and sheltered, creating a heat sink for these hot-weather-loving plants. In addition, container-grown eggplants are seldom bothered by flea beetles, Colorado potato beetles, or verticillium wilt, a common eggplant disease.

Start with a large pot at least 12 to 15 inches in diameter. A dark-colored container will absorb heat and warm the soil, which makes eggplants happy. Fill with a good-quality potting mix, adding some compost and slow-release organic fertilizer as well.

Pick a compact, container-friendly cultivar like 'Little Prince', 'Bride', 'Rosa Bianca', or 'Little Fingers'. Insert a cage or stake at planting time to support the seedlings as they grow.

Consistent water is key to high-quality, nonbitter eggplants. This is even more important for container-grown plants, which can be prone to drying out. Check soil moisture daily and water deeply. Mulching the soil with straw or shredded leaves will reduce the need to water.

Fertilize every 2 weeks, even if you worked granular organic fertilizer into the soil before planting.

growing great eggplants

> Eggplants have a reputation for being fussy, but they're really quite easy, as long as they're given fertile, well-drained soil that has been prewarmed (with a sheet of black plastic) and enriched with compost or aged manure, as well as lots of sun and heat.

> Choose varieties that will have plenty of time to mature in your climate, start seeds indoors around 8 weeks before the last expected spring frost, and provide bottom heat to speed up germination.

> Our uncertain spring weather can be tough on eggplant seedlings, and I've found that erecting a mini hoop tunnel over my eggplant bed can mean the difference between success and failure.

> If transplanted too early, the heat-loving seedlings will sulk or be set back by cold weather. I usually wait until a week or two after my last expected spring frost.

> If your garden has been plagued by pesky flea beetles in the past, you may want to drape a lightweight insect barrier over the seedlings immediately after planting. Remove row covers when flowers emerge so pollination can occur.

> To avoid bitter fruits, water plants regularly, supplying 1 to 2 inches of water per week. Avoid wetting the foliage, which can spread disease, and instead water the base of the plant.

> Side-dress occasionally with a balanced organic fertilizer. Eggplant are heavy feeders, but avoid nitrogen-rich fertilizers, as they will produce vigorous plants with few flowers or fruit.

> Pick eggplant when the skin is glossy and the fruits are slightly immature. This is when they will offer the highest-quality flavor, fewest seeds, and thinnest skin.

like arugula?

try these
spicy
greens!

'Catalogna
Special'
dandelion

'Garnet
Stem'
dandelion

'Green
Wave'
mustard

'Nozawana'
turnip
green

If you love the peppery bite of arugula, you'll want to try 'Green Spray' mibuna, a fast-growing Asian green with smooth, narrow leaves.

A rugula is our salad green of choice, thriving in both garden beds and cold frames for almost 12 months of the year. We love the peppery bite of its distinctive lobed foliage and its ridiculously quick growth; in spring, a seeding of baby arugula can be ready to harvest in as few as 30 days!

In winter, our cold frames are filled with 'Sylvetta' arugula — often sold as "wild" arugula but actually a totally different species. It has a strong flavor and finely divided leaves and is slower to grow, ready to harvest in about 60 days. Most significantly, though, it's far more cold tolerant than garden arugula is; we harvest it all winter long from our frames.

'Sylvetta' isn't the only arugula imposter in our garden. If you crave the bite of garden-fresh arugula, you might also be interested in turnip greens, Asian greens like mustard and mizuna, or even Italian dandelions (not true dandelions), which have a sharp, peppery flavor that's suggestive of arugula.

growing great greens

> Growing in pots gives you the option of moving the greens to a shady spot if the spring weather turns unseasonably warm; a bit of shade will delay bolting (going to flower) and stretch out the harvest.

> Greens grow quickest and taste best when grown under ideal conditions. For most greens, this means full sun, rich organic soil, and a steady supply of moisture.

> In spring, direct sow seeds as soon as the soil can be worked. If you have the protection of a cold frame, you can sow even earlier.

> For direct-sown baby greens, scatter seed in foot-wide bands, trying to space the seed at least an inch apart. Thin excess seedlings in a week or two, nibbling on the tiny shoots as you work. Expect a harvest of baby greens in just 30 to 50 days. To ensure a nonstop supply, succession plant every 2 to 3 weeks. To harvest, pluck individual leaves from the plants when they are 2 to 4 inches in length, or slice off plants at soil level.

> For larger plants, sow seed an inch apart, eventually thinning to 6 inches. In my raised beds, I practice intensive planting, transplanting seedlings in a 6-inch grid pattern for the most efficient use of space. Mature loose heads can be harvested a few weeks after baby greens. Harvest the entire plant by slicing it off at the soil level.

> As the greens grow, water regularly and remove any weeds. Mulch the soil with straw or shredded leaves to conserve moisture and suppress weeds.

If salad crops are grown with too little water, they can bolt prematurely; their flavor also declines. Radish and turnip greens, as well as mustards and dandelion, quickly turn bitter in hot, dry weather.

> To reduce pressure from pests like flea beetles, top just-planted beds with a floating row cover in spring. Handpick slugs, particularly in times of wet weather. Autumn-grown greens are out of sync with the lifecycle of many spring pests and are less frequently bothered by bugs.

> Fast-growing greens can also be used as an inter-crop between slower-growing vegetables like kale, broccoli, cabbage, and onions. Just sprinkle seed in the spaces between the later crops and by the time the greens are harvested about 4 to 6 weeks later, the slower-growing vegetables are ready for the space.

> Start fall plantings indoors under lights. Starting the seeds of crops like mizuna, mustard, celtuce, and loose-leaf Asian cabbages indoors decreases the amount of water needed to coddle the greens in the seed-to-seedling stage, eliminates the pest pressure that young seedlings can face in the garden, and helps the crop establish quickly, reducing the time needed from planting to harvest.

> As the temperature plunges in fall, cover beds of greens with a row cover or mini hoop tunnel to extend the harvest. The flavor of certain crops, like turnip greens, improves in cool weather.

TRY THIS! mizuna

THE DETAILS

A.K.A.: *Brassica rapa* subsp. *nipposinica*

DAYS TO MATURITY: 40 days

HAILS FROM: East Asia

VARIETY TO TRY: 'Red Kingdom'

I FIRST DISCOVERED MIZUNA when I began experimenting with season extension and cold-season harvesting more than a decade ago. It was an immediate standout, shrugging off the frigid winter weather to provide a mild peppery punch to mixed salads, homemade sushi, stir-fries, and sandwiches. Come spring, I planted it again and discovered it's also heat tolerant, lasting well into autumn and, unlike my flea beetle–ridden arugula, was bothered by few pests.

Flavor-wise, mizuna packs less heat than mustard greens and tastes like a cabbage-arugula hybrid. No surprise there, as mizuna is a member of the sizable cabbage family. It also falls firmly into the category of edible ornamental. The plants form unruly rosettes of deeply cut, feathery leaves held on thin white stems. There is also a purple form, with leaves edged in bronze purple. Both make excellent container plants — I like to mix them with my annual flowers in big pots — but they can also be used as a low-growing edge at the front of flower or shrub beds.

BUZZ CUTS AND EDIBLE BLOOMS

The easiest way to harvest mizuna is to remove the outer leaves of the plant, allowing the center to keep growing. You can also treat this like a cut-and-come-again crop, giving the plant a buzz cut just above ground level. Leave a 1- to 2-inch stub, and water in some fish emulsion after harvesting. The stub will quickly regrow for subsequent harvests.

Eventually the plants will throw up some pretty (and edible) broccoli-like flower buds, which open into cheerful yellow blooms. Eat the bud clusters like broccoli or let them open and sprinkle the flowers on salads, pasta, fish, and chicken dishes.

IF YOU LIKE MIZUNA, YOU'LL LOVE MIBUNA

Mibuna is a lesser-known Asian green but has a similar growth style as mizuna, forming dense clusters of narrow, almost grassy foliage. The leaf edge is smooth with no serration, and one bite will tell you that mibuna packs more heat than the milder mizuna. Grow and harvest it as you would mizuna. My favorite variety is 'Green Spray', a Japanese hybrid that thrives in both spring and fall and also persists into winter when protected by a cold frame or mini hoop tunnel.

'Green Spray' mibuna

'Red Giant' mustard

Must-Have Mustards

LIKE MIZUNA, MUSTARD is a popular Asian green and a cabbage cousin that is both easy and quick to grow, is productive, and thrives in both full sun and partial shade. Most gardeners will want to grow mustard for baby greens, which are far less spicy than full-grown plants.

Because there is such diversity in leaf color, shape, and texture, I like to plant mustards in small vignettes in our vegetable garden, playing with different patterns and combinations — alternating rows, checkerboards, diagonal stripes, and so on. Within weeks, the plants begin to fill in and the patterns emerge. The various leaf colors and textures will add welcome heat and visual interest to your salad bowls and stir-fries.

THREE GREAT MUSTARDS TO TRY

'GOLDEN FRILLS'. Oh, how I love this gorgeous green! The flavor is pleasantly pungent, and the fast-growing plants form low mounds of neon green frills. It's an outstanding choice for edible landscaping. But even when planted alone — such as in a window box — it's very eye-catching.

'RUBY STREAKS'. Another looker, 'Ruby Streaks' is the first "frilly"-type mustard I tried in our garden, and I still adore it. The two-toned leaves are an attractive combination of green and purply red and have a mild mustardy bite. Tuck it in pots or ornamental gardens to add a touch of "purple power!"

'RED GIANT'. This is one of my favorite cold-frame crops for winter harvesting, and I intentionally plant it in mid-autumn so that it will be baby-size for most of the winter. This is considered the spiciest of the mustards, but the smaller leaves have less kick than their full-grown counterparts. Of course, a few plants will end up larger — and spicier — than intended, but fear not, as the zing is tempered with a quick stir-fry.

MICRO OR MEGA

Mustard can be harvested at any time, from a microgreen to a mature plant. Our first harvest comes when we thin the plants in early spring. These tiny seedlings are usually only 1 or 2 inches tall, and we gobble them up as we thin them.

Generally, I prefer to harvest mustard as a baby green, when the leaves are about 2 to 4 inches long. If you keep picking the outer leaves, the center of the plant will continue to yield for many weeks. Large leaves, sometimes a foot or more long, can be sliced up for stir-fries or sautéed with a bit of chicken stock and garlic. Tasty!

THE DETAILS

A.K.A.: *Brassica juncea*

DAYS TO MATURITY: 21 days for baby greens, 40 days to maturity

HAILS FROM: Central Asia

VARIETIES TO TRY: See below.

'Ruby Streaks' mustard

'Golden Frills' mustard

TRY THIS!
Italian Dandelion

I KNOW WHAT YOU'RE THINKING: "Dandelions? Why on earth would I want to grow dandelions?" Yet, before you flip to the next page, let me point out that Italian dandelions are not actually dandelions. They're a card-carrying member of the chicory family, which includes salad favorites like endive and radicchio. They're also a staple ingredient in Italian cuisine, where they are called *catalogna frastagliata*. (Try to say it out loud; doesn't it sound so much better than "dandelion"?) It means "jagged catalonia," a reference to the toothy leaves and the type of chicory (catalonia).

The first time I grew them, I'll admit that it felt a bit funny planting dandelion seeds in my vegetable garden ("What have I done?!"), but my Lebanese mother-in-law was thrilled to be given bunches of the deep green leaves just 7 weeks later. She quickly chopped them into bite-size pieces and then lightly sautéed them with garlic, olive oil, and a liberal dash of salt and pepper. Delicious!

Many gardeners, including my mother-in-law, also enjoy them raw in salads, but be warned that the uncooked leaves have a potent bitter flavor that you might say is an acquired taste. If lettuce is your idea of an adventurous green, you might want to ease your way into eating Italian dandelion. When eaten raw in salads, choose young, less bitter leaves and consider making them part of a bowl of mixed greens. You might find mature leaves too strong to eat alone. Cooking mutes some of the bitterness. So does blanching before cooking. Blanch mature leaves in boiling water for 1 to 2 minutes before sautéing them with aromatics.

FRIEND OR WEED?

It's true that the leaves of Italian dandelions do resemble their weedy relations, but if you look closer, you'll see that these have larger leaves and form attractive upright rosettes. Those rosettes can grow 12 to 15 inches tall but should be harvested when they are less than 10 inches. The deep green leaves contrast nicely with the white midribs, but there is also a red variety that I like to grow called 'Garnet Stem' that has unusual dark red leaf stalks.

'Garnet Stem'
Italian dandelion

Italian dandelion

Plants that are left in the ground will eventually produce edible sky-blue flowers, which can be added to salads (like the leaves, they have a mild bitterness) or used to make wine.

EDIBLE FROM TIP TO ROOT

For salads, start harvesting baby leaves about 5 weeks after germination. Pick individual leaves for cooked greens, or harvest the entire rosette by slicing it off at soil level. The stump will regrow and offer several future harvests. A little fish emulsion at this point will hasten the subsequent harvest.

At some point, you'll probably want to pull the roots to clear the bed, and if you're feeling ambitious, you can also use the roots to make chicory coffee. After washing and chopping, the roots can be slow-roasted in an oven and then ground into little bits for "coffee'" grounds. This isn't a wimpy brew, however, and has a powerful bitterness that you may find turns out to be an acquired taste.

THE DETAILS

A.K.A.: Chicory, *Cichorium intybus*

DAYS TO MATURITY: 48 days

HAILS FROM: Mediterranean

VARIETY TO TRY: 'Garnet Stem'

Turnip Greens

THE DETAILS

A.K.A.: *Brassica rapa* var. *rapifera*

DAYS TO MATURITY: 30–40 days

HAILS FROM: Mediterranean to Asia

VARIETIES TO TRY: 'Hakurei', 'Nozawana', 'Seven Top'

I'M A SUCKER FOR TURNIP GREENS. In fact, I think I prefer the greens to the turnips! Typically the best-quality turnip tops come from the varieties bred specifically for greens — such as 'All Top', 'Seven Top', and 'Nozawana', but I also love the tasty greens from the popular Japanese variety 'Hakurei'.

Turnip tops are extremely fast growing, ready to pick in about 4 to 5 weeks. They're packed with nutrition and are high in vitamins K, A, and C, as well as manganese, copper, fiber, and calcium. Their flavor is similar to arugula, as well as that of Asian greens like mustard and mizuna. Plants grown under stressful conditions — too little water, too much heat — will be more pungent.

Turnip greens grow well in containers, window boxes, and planters. Growing in pots gives you the option of moving the greens to a shady spot if the spring weather turns unseasonably warm, which will delay bolting and stretch out the harvest.

The prime time for turnip tops is really in the fall, when the cooler temperatures and shorter days prevent bolting and sweeten the leaves. I start sowing in late summer, continuing to plant fresh seed every few weeks until mid-October. For a baby crop, sow seed thickly in garden beds and cold frames. Turnip greens are tolerant of cold temperatures and can be harvested until late autumn and even into winter if they have some protection.

START PICKING

With dense plantings of baby turnip tops, I begin picking when the leaves are 2 to 3 inches long. This is a great technique for a cold frame, window box, or large planter and allows you to get a large harvest from a small space. Of course, I also grow them in garden beds, planting on 6-inch centers, and we harvest these by continually pulling the outer leaves. This allows the middle of the plants to continue growing. You can also pick an entire plant by slicing it off at ground level when it reaches a harvestable size.

TOP TOPS!

'HAKUREI' (38 days). Most gardeners grow this farmers' market favorite for the creamy white roots, but for me that's a bonus crop; the real prize is the deep green foliage. We chop the tops into bite-size pieces and eat them raw with a simple drizzle of olive oil, a squirt of lemon juice, and a sprinkle of salt.

'NOZAWANA' (40 days). This Japanese selection is grown for its dark green leaves and pale green stalks. In Asia, it's often pickled.

'SEVEN TOP' (45 days). Bred for leaf production, this variety doesn't develop edible roots. If left unchecked, the dark foliage will grow up to 18 inches tall, but I'd suggest picking the leaves when they are 6 to 10 inches for best eating quality. This heirloom is also tolerant of cold weather and can be grown for late-fall and winter harvesting.

'Hakurei'

like lettuce?

try these!

Tokyo bekana

Mâche

Celtuce

Minutina

Celtuce foliage tastes something like romaine lettuce, but its long, crunchy stem is really what you're after.

L ettuce is a classic salad green, but who says salads have to be all about lettuce, anyway? Expanding your repertoire beyond lettuce introduces you to plants that may offer features that lettuce doesn't — like extreme winter hardiness or summer heat tolerance. Or perhaps you'll stumble on a plant that offers a dual harvest. For example, celtuce offers tender early foliage and late crunchy stems.

TRY THIS!
Crunchy Celtuce

CELTUCE IS A RARE VEGETABLE in North American gardens but a staple in the markets and gardens of Asia. A member of the lettuce family, this nonheading plant is named for its similarities to celery and lettuce, as well as for the fact that it offers a dual harvest: tender early leaves eventually followed by a long, dense, crunchy stem in late summer.

Fellow fans of celtuce have described its flavor to me as "nutty," "like asparagus," or "like rice." I'll leave you to draw your own conclusions, but I find the mild taste of the immature leaves comparable to that of romaine lettuce. The large stems, which will grow 8 to 12 inches tall and up to 2 inches wide, are ready to cut in late summer. They are excellent chopped or cut into coins for roasting or for stir-fries and stews.

THE TRANSFORMER
Celtuce is not difficult to grow. It's actually quite fun to watch it transform from a low rosette of lettucelike leaves into a tall stem plant. The process is much like that of lettuce when it bolts, but the eventual stem will be thicker and woodier. Celtuce will grow in most soils — even tolerating clay — but it does best in friable, well-amended soil, so dig in some compost or aged manure before planting.

I've had luck direct seeding, but because slugs like to nibble on the just-germinated seedlings, I prefer to start the seeds indoors under grow lights 4 to 5 weeks before I plan on moving the plants out to the garden. If you want to direct seed, plant the seeds an inch apart as soon as the soil can be worked in early spring. Celtuce germinates best in cool temperatures (50 to 60°F/10 to 15°C), and waiting until the weather is warmer will reduce germination rates. Germination can take 14 to 21 days.

Once the plants are growing well, thin them to 8 inches, or plant seedlings on 8-inch centers if growing in a grid pattern. Don't forget to eat those tiny thinnings; they're delicious as microgreens. Gardeners in warmer regions — Zone 6 and above — may wish to grow celtuce in partial or afternoon shade. This will reduce leaf bitterness. Celtuce is relatively resistant to common garden pests, besides deer and the occasional nibble by slugs or snails.

THE DETAILS
A.K.A.: Chinese lettuce, stem lettuce, asparagus lettuce, *wo sun*, *Lactuca sativa* var. *asparagina*

DAYS TO MATURITY: 45 days for greens, 90 days for stems

HAILS FROM: Southern China

VARIETIES TO TRY: None

HARVESTING LEAF AND STEM

SPRING LEAVES. The first celtuce harvest comes from the lettucelike leaves in early spring, about 5 to 6 weeks from seeding or a month after transplanting. Those young leaves wilt quickly after harvest, so pick when you're ready to eat.

As summer progresses and the stem begins to grow and thicken, the leaves will turn bitter, like lettuce that has bolted. The culprit is the milky white sap — you'll see it ooze from the bottom of the just-picked leaves.

FALL STEMS. The stem will be ready to pick after about 3 months from planting, when it's 8 to 10 inches tall and has thickened to about 1½ to 2 inches. If left unharvested, the stem will continue to grow, often reaching 3 to 4 feet, but the eating quality will be far diminished.

To harvest, cut the stem at soil level. To prep it for eating, peel the thick outer skin, which contains more of that bitter sap. The "heart" of the stem, or the inner core, offers the best eating: you'll find it to be crispy and dense, and not stringy like celery. Chop the core into coins or chunks and add it to soups, stews, curries, stir-fries, and other Asian-inspired dishes. The stem retains a pleasing crunch, even when cooked. You can eat celtuce raw, but pick young stems, which are only slightly bitter. Mature stems will be very bitter. If you want to prep the stem ahead of time, just peel and store in the fridge in plastic bags. It will keep for at least a week.

TRY THIS!
Mild Minutina

THE DETAILS

A.K.A.: Buckshorn plantain, sweetgrass, *Plantago coronopus*

DAYS TO MATURITY: 50 days

HAILS FROM: Europe

VARIETIES TO TRY: None

MINUTINA HAS BEEN a popular edible green for centuries, particularly in Italy where it is known as *erba stella* ("star grass"). It forms low, grassy clumps made up of narrow, serrated leaves that resemble antlers — hence its alternate name, buckshorn plantain. It adds a delicate texture to garden beds and makes a pretty planting partner for the larger, bolder foliage of lettuce. Minutina has a mild, sweet, almost nutty flavor and a crunchy texture.

Like dandelions, plantain is a common lawn weed. You might therefore wonder why I'm suggesting you consider planting it in your vegetable garden. Let me stop you there. This plantain is a completely different species from the one that plagues your lawn. That one is *Plantago major* and, although also edible, is definitely not suited to your cultivated garden. Why? The plants can produce more than 10,000 seeds per year, quickly overwhelming your growing space.

LOOKS LIKE GRASS . . .

Minutina can be direct-seeded in prepared garden beds or started indoors in early spring. I prefer to sow it under my grow lights in late March, moving the small plants to the garden 4 to 5 weeks later. When newly germinated, the seedlings look very much like grass; the first year I grew them, I did mistake them for grassy weeds and pulled them all out! Now I start them indoors, giving them a time to size up a bit before they move to the garden.

Like most salad crops, the best-quality harvest comes when the leaves are picked slightly immature, about 4 to 6 inches long. You can harvest it as a cut-and-come-again crop, but it's very slow to regrow; you're better off starting a few pots of seeds indoors for succession planting. Harvest by picking the individual leaves as needed or cutting the whole plant at soil level. By early summer, the plants will begin to flower, sending up subtle green flower spikes, which diminishes the leaf quality. The unusual blooms are edible and can be added to salads as well.

SEED SAVING AND WINTER HARVEST

The seeds are easy to save for future plantings. Just gather the ripe seed heads and spread them on a paper plate or piece of newspaper indoors. Allow them to dry for a week or two before rubbing them between your fingers, over a paper plate, to release the tiny seeds. Store the seeds in envelopes until you're ready to plant.

Minutina is also a good candidate for winter harvesting and can be sown in cold frames, beneath the shelter of a mini hoop tunnel, or in greenhouses in early autumn. The foliage is very cold tolerant, and the succulent leaves add a welcome crunch to winter salads.

Minutina

TRY THIS!
Tasty Tokyo Bekana

THE DETAILS

A.K.A.: *Brassica rapa*
var. *chinensis*

DAYS TO MATURITY:
21 days for baby,
45 days for mature

HAILS FROM: China

VARIETIES TO TRY:
None, but if you like
Tokyo bekana, try
fun jen, another easy-
to-grow, nonheading
Chinese cabbage that
looks and tastes like
lettuce.

AT FIRST GLANCE, Tokyo bekana looks like a type of lettuce. It forms pretty clumps with leaves that are spring green, like 'Black Seeded Simpson' lettuce, and also slightly crinkled and waved around the edges. But it's not a lettuce — it's a loose-headed Chinese cabbage that reaches maturity just 6 weeks from seeding.

It doesn't just *look* like lettuce, it also *tastes* like lettuce, with a pleasing crunch and a mild, sweet flavor that lasts even as the plants mature. In fact, I doubt that even the biggest salad snob will notice that Tokyo bekana isn't legitimate lettuce when mixed with other baby greens. At maturity, the full-size leaves look more like those of Chinese cabbage with large crunchy stems, which can be chopped up with the leaves and gently stir-fried.

Direct seed in amended garden beds or containers in mid-spring, just a week or two before the last expected frost, and again in late summer for fall harvest. Like many greens, I sow it in bands 3 to 4 inches wide, thinning a few weeks later to a 6-inch spacing. All those thinnings make an excellent baby salad or can be added to wraps and sandwiches. Protect your plants from slugs and flea beetles, which also love this hardy crop, and water often to keep flavor and leaf quality high.

Begin picking about 3 weeks after seeding by thinning plants or plucking the outer leaves from the growing rosettes. Entire plants can also be sliced off at soil level, leaving a 2-inch stub to regrow. I like to stir-fry entire young plants (3 to 4 inches tall) as you would baby pak choi.

Tokyo bekana

Mâche for All Seasons

Mâche

MÂCHE IS A COLD-SEASON SUPERSTAR!
It's also among the most versatile of the salad greens, thriving not only in winter but also in spring, summer, and autumn. The tender, nutty, mild foliage never turns bitter. And the small rosettes — made up of a whorl of tiny, spoon-shaped leaves — have made this a trendy salad ingredient in restaurants and at farmers' markets. Mâche is typically rather pricey to buy, which makes growing it even more worthwhile.

There isn't a day of the year that I can't venture out to my backyard to pick mâche — and I haven't sown seeds in years! How many vegetables can make this claim? It's not perennial, but because it reseeds so promiscuously, baby plants pop up everywhere. In autumn, I dig up the babies and move them where I want them, planting them in a grid formation to get the most out of my space.

MÂCHE THROUGH THE YEAR

In my garden, the first harvest of the year comes in early January from the cold frames, which shelter the plants and allow easy harvesting until the snow melts in late winter. When that snow does finally melt, it reveals perfect mâche rosettes that had been lying hidden all winter long.

We continue to harvest mâche into spring, with any remaining plants turning to seed production in midsummer. When the seed is ripe, I pull up the plants, shaking them over the beds and cold frames where we want a fall and winter crop. Done! Soon the seeds germinate, and the cycle begins again.

If you're new to mâche and planting for the first time, look for a sunny site with well-drained soil and amend with compost or aged manure. You can direct seed in the garden as soon as the frost has left the soil in early spring, but I prefer mâche for a fall and winter crop. Let a few overwintered plants go to seed for self-sowing, but also sow fresh seed in late August to ensure a good cold-season harvest. When planting, space the seeds an inch apart, but eventually thin to 4 to 6 inches.

THE PERFECT BITE

When full grown, mâche plants are only 2 to 4 inches across — a perfect bite! Harvest them by slicing the entire plant at ground level with a sharp knife; place the rosettes gently in a bowl. After a quick rinse, we toss the whole mâche plants with a simple vinaigrette. They can also be used as an edible base for chicken and fish dishes or as a garnish.

THE DETAILS

A.K.A.: Corn salad, lamb's lettuce, *Valerianella locusta*

DAYS TO MATURITY: 50–60 days

HAILS FROM: Europe

VARIETIES TO TRY:
There are two types of mâche: large seeded and small seeded. Small-seeded types like 'Vit' are generally planted for cool- and cold-season harvesting. The large-seeded mâche varieties, like 'Medallion', are more heat tolerant and can be sown in early spring for late-spring and summer harvesting.

Mâche is easy to grow, productive, and seldom bothered by pests and diseases. Plus, it's very nutritious, with three times more vitamin C than lettuce.

WHY GROW ORDINARY KALE?

'Bear Necessities'

WITH KALE, THERE SEEMS TO BE no in-between, you either love it or you hate it. I'm firmly in the "love it" camp, but that comes with a few conditions. First of all, I love it in autumn and winter, after the frost has kissed the leaves and turned them sweet. Midsummer kale? No thanks, I'll wait. I also love kale when it's grown as a baby crop, and the young leaves are supertender.

In my region, most garden centers offer one variety of kale — 'Red Russian'. So if I want to take advantage of some of the more uncommon varieties in the kale palette, I need to grow them from seed myself. Here are a few I've fallen madly in love with.

'RAINBOW LACINATO' (65 days). This is a beautiful, tasty kale created by Frank Morton, who crossed the popular 'Lacinato' with the cold-tolerant 'Redbor'. The result is a plant with gorgeous multicolored foliage — in shades of red, purple, green, and greenish blue — with excellent cold tolerance. This partially perennial kale usually persists for several years in my garden. I've had it grow 4 feet tall, but in a slightly warmer region, I expect it could get even taller! It's also super productive, and the curly leaves tend to be more resistant to cabbageworms than 'Lacinato' and 'Red Russian'.

'BEAR NECESSITIES' (60 days). Here is a fabulous collection of kales with deeply divided, intensely frilled, sometimes purple-tinged leaves. They add beauty and texture to the veggie patch and edible interest to your containers. 'Bear Necessities' can also be grown for fall and winter harvesting, but it should be protected with a mini hoop tunnel or cold frame in winter. The variety came about when plant breeder

'Rainbow Lacinato'

Tim Peters are crossed mizuna with Russian and Siberian kales.

KOSMIC (perennial; hardy to Zone 6 or colder with protection). Unlike most varieties, this Netherlands-bred kale doesn't produce seed; it's propagated through root cuttings and sold as young plants. What makes KOSMIC kale so special? Several reasons: First, it's reliably perennial. Second, it has variegated foliage — blue-green leaves edged in cream. They've also got a slight wave to them and are produced in profusion on the tall stems. And it tastes great! It's an edible plant with ornamental flair.

KALETTES. Not quite a kale, but not quite a Brussels sprout, KALETTES are a recent introduction from Tozer Seeds of Britain. Each ruffly whorl of purple-green foliage is produced along the mature plant stalk, in the same manner as Brussels sprouts. The flavor is similar to the parent plants: mildly nutty, and a bit sweet, especially after a few autumn frosts. KALETTES are very easy to grow but are long-season crops and take at least 110 days to mature. Give them fertile soil and plenty of sunshine.

like asparagus?

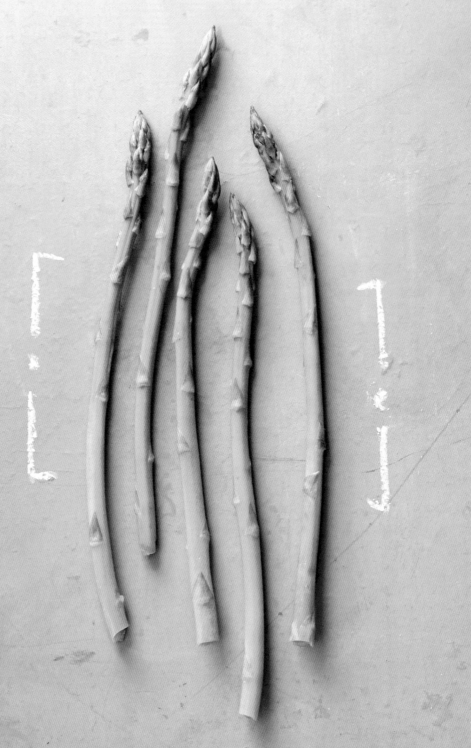

try these taste-alikes!

Hosta
shoots

Humor me for a second, and let's think outside the vegetable garden. Maybe all the way to the shady perennial border? When I think of crops that have an asparagus-like flavor, two come to mind: hosta shoots and asparagus peas.

In North America, hostas are a traditional garden perennial, but I would guess that very few of us have foraged for those tender spring shoots. As for asparagus peas, I prefer to grow them for their fabulous foliage and flowers over their edible small pods that hint of asparagus.

Yet if nothing but asparagus will do, consider planting a few of the unusual heirloom varieties available through seed catalogs. 'Precoce d'Argenteuil' is a beauty with light green spears and large contrasting purple scales. Or grow a proven hybrid like 'Purple Passion', a purple-speared variety with an exceptional sweet flavor.

(the fancy word for hosta shoots); leaves and leaf stalks; and flowers.

The first time my family tried them, we ventured out in early spring, when the tightly furled shoots were about 6 to 7 inches tall. Slicing them at ground level, we brought our bounty indoors for a quick rinse, and soon they were sizzling in a frying pan with a little chopped garlic and soy sauce. The flavor was green, similar to asparagus, but also with hints of spinach — very good! And I can tell you that hosta is far easier to grow than asparagus!

SHADY SUBSTITUTES

Hostas thrive in many conditions, but most are well suited to partial shade. Give them decent soil, working in some compost to help aid moisture retention. Hostas grow best — and *taste* best — when they have ample moisture. They're generally pest-free, but they are a favorite of slugs and deer. They can also become overgrown and benefit from being dug up and divided every 3 to 5 years.

HARVESTING HOSTONS

The harvest begins in early spring, as the snow retreats from the hosta bed. When the hostons emerge, slice them just above the crown, before the leaves unfurl. You don't want to weaken the plant, so don't harvest more than a quarter of the shoots in any given year.

Hostons can be stir-fried, sautéed, steamed, roasted, sliced raw in salads, dipped in tempura and fried, or sliced and added to pasta or lasagna. Young leaves can be cooked like spinach, but the older leaves are fibrous and less palatable. Flower petals add color to salads and can be used as an edible garnish.

THE DETAILS

A.K.A.: *Hosta montana*

DAYS TO MATURITY: Perennial, Zones 3 to 9

HAILS FROM: Japan

VARIETIES TO TRY: All varieties of *H. montana* are edible.

TRY THIS!
hosta shoots

IN JAPAN, CERTAIN SPECIES of *Hosta*, like *H. montana*, are grown as a vegetable crop called *urui*. Here in North America, most of us aren't eating our hostas, but if you love asparagus, you should give it a try! Hostas offer a range of edible parts: hostons

Asparagus Peas

I'VE TALKED TO GARDENERS who adore this quirky crop and others who detest it, so it seems, like cilantro, it's either love or hate. The name "asparagus peas" likely comes from the hint of asparagus in their flavor. But it's also said to originate from their common method of preparation: blanched and sautéed in butter. When picked very young, I find the four-sided, winged pods do have a hint of asparagus as well as a sharp flavor (which, if you like it, you can mute somewhat blanching or boiling for 10 minutes).

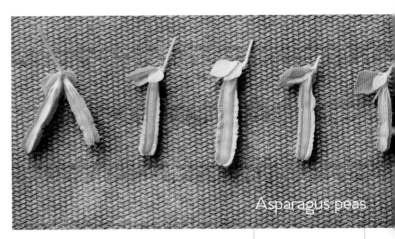

Asparagus peas

I have to be honest, though; I'm actually not a big fan of *eating* asparagus peas. I do admire them, though! I love their low, sprawling plant habit and the gorgeous brick-red flowers that precede the funky pods. They look spectacular when grown in containers or at the front of a flower border, and they will bloom all summer long if watered regularly.

LOW GROWERS

These are not a common listing in catalogs, but many heirloom-seed companies do offer asparagus peas. They can be mistaken for the tropical crop, Hunan winged beans (*Psophocarpus tetragonolobus*, see page 68), but asparagus peas have a much different growth habit and flavor.

Asparagus peas can be direct-seeded after the danger of frost has passed in Zone 7 and warmer, but in Zones 5 and 6, I recommend starting the seeds indoors in late March. In my garden, I sow them in 4-inch pots and move the seedlings to the garden in early June, spacing them about a foot apart. Alternatively, you can plant them in containers or pots on a deck or patio. Whether planted in the garden or in pots, they'll need full sun and appreciate some compost or aged manure mixed into their soil prior to planting.

The low-lying plants only grow about 10 inches tall, but they cover 1½ to 2 feet of horizontal space. If the weather turns cold after planting, cover the seedlings with a row cover. Once the summer is reliably warm, expect the plants to quickly fill their space.

PICK YOUR FUNKY PODS

Many crops offer the best harvest when picked young, and asparagus peas are no exception. Although they'll grow up to 3 inches long, you must harvest the pods before they are an inch long; otherwise, they become tough, fibrous, and bitter. Blanch the immature pods for about 10 minutes and then add them to stir-fries.

THE DETAILS

A.K.A.: Winged pea, *Lotus tetragonolobus*

DAYS TO MATURITY: 70 days

HAILS FROM: Africa

VARIETIES TO TRY: None

like spinach?

try these greens!

New Zealand spinach

Orach

Green amaranth

Purple amaranth

Molokhia

Magenta spreen

Sweet potato leaf

Tricolor amaranth

Let's get something straight: I've got nothing against spinach. In fact, I'd say it's the most versatile vegetable in our garden. We eat it raw in salads, and we toss handfuls of homegrown spinach in soups, pastas, curry, quiche, omelets, casseroles, and, my favorite treat, spinach-artichoke dip.

Spinach is a three-season crop, growing best in cool weather. It's among the first vegetables sown in our early spring garden and one of the last to be seeded in our cold frames in late October. Ideally, I'd love to have garden-fresh spinach every day of the year, but spinach quickly bolts when spring turns to summer, reducing its quality and flavor.

It's this tendency to bolt that encouraged me to seek out alternative greens that could stand in for spinach during the heat of summer. I was happily surprised to find not one but many crops that made excellent substitutes: sweet potato leaves, amaranth, magenta spreen, New Zealand spinach, molokhia, orach, and more. I even discovered some perennial crops, like "habby," better known as hablitizia, which offers a dual harvest of tender spring shoots followed by its spinachlike leafy foliage.

Soon I was looking for greens that would outcompete spinach not just in summer but also in winter. Enter tatsoi, an Asian crop that is incredibly cold tolerant, shrugging off our coldest winter weather. Of course, I still grow spinach, usually several varieties at any one time, but my garden now offers a range of greens for raw eating or cooked dishes.

Many of the crops you're about to meet may not be as well known as spinach, but that doesn't diminish their amazing attributes. All are easy-to-grow, highly productive plants with the added bonus of dramatic, ornamental foliage and/or flowers, and some even produce edible seeds.

TRY THIS!
Magenta Spreen

THE DETAILS

A.K.A.: Tree spinach, giant lamb's quarters, *Chenopodium giganteum*

DAYS TO MATURITY: 30 days for baby greens, 50 for full-size leaves

HAILS FROM: India

VARIETIES TO TRY: None

MAGENTA SPREEN IS ONE of those edibles that falls into the category of "almost too pretty to eat." Grown for its foliage, this Asian native and quinoa cousin yields a heavy crop of soft green foliage highlighted by a bold splash of magenta pink at the center of each shoot. From a distance, the bright pink patina pops, but up close, it's simply stunning — an iridescent powdery coating that dusts the foliage.

Magenta spreen is more than a pretty face, however. In my garden, it's a salad superstar, outproducing both spinach and chard, and boasting excellent heat, pest, and disease resistance. Unlike spinach, which sometimes seems to bolt mere weeks after planting, magenta spreen is made of sterner stuff and quickly fills its allotted space with tender leaves. It's also super speedy and ready for a first harvest just 4 to 5 weeks from seeding. Allow the plants to continue growing, and they'll eventually reach a height of 8 feet and be topped by intense purple-pink flower spikes.

GROWING GREAT SPREEN

Introduced to North American gardeners by Dr. Alan Kapuler of Peace Seeds, magenta spreen is very easy to grow and can be planted in both gardens and containers. Because of its unusual color combination, it's a good candidate for edible landscaping, so feel free to tuck it between ornamental plants in beds and borders.

Magenta spreen prefers a sunny site in the garden with decent soil. Direct sow the tiny seeds as soon as the soil can be worked in early spring. The cold, wet weather will help break seed dormancy and hasten germination. If you're giving the plants a head start indoors, sow in pots and place in the refrigerator for about a week to encourage germination.

As the seedlings emerge in the garden, thin them to 3 inches apart (eating the tasty thinnings, of course!). For larger plants, allow a foot between each seedling. If you'd rather have young greens than mature plants, succession sow fresh seed every 3 to 4 weeks to ensure a nonstop supply of tender leaves.

Like most plants, magenta spreen also responds to pinching, so if you're allowing your plants to mature, give them a quick pinch when they're about a foot tall. This will encourage branching and boost yield. Don't forget to eat the parts you pinched.

When the flowers emerge in late summer, crop quality declines. To keep the harvest going, pinch out flower buds as they appear.

As one of its common names suggests, magenta spreen is a member of the lamb's quarters family. And like its weedy namesake, if you allow those gorgeous flowers to form and set seeds, you'll find it rather (ahem) promiscuous. However, prompt removal of the spent blooms will easily prevent the appearance of unwelcome seedlings the following spring.

FROM MICROCROP TO MATURE PLANT

As a food crop, magenta spreen is incredibly useful and can be harvested at all stages of its lifecycle. We even grow it as a winter microgreen under our grow lights, scissor harvesting the tiny plants after just a week or two. Ideally, however, it's best as a young green, harvested when the plants are just 6 to 8 inches tall and the foliage is very tender. Mature plants are also edible, but by that point, the tough stems will need to be removed. Once flowering begins, the greens lose quality.

Use mild-flavored magenta spreen in place of spinach in your favorite raw and cooked dishes. Like spinach and chard, it does contain oxalic acid, which can inhibit the absorption of calcium and iron from the plant (it doesn't affect that of other foods). Those prone to kidney stones may want to avoid eating large quantities of oxalic acid–rich foods (though keep in mind that oxalic acid is reduced with cooking).

Magenta spreen

Amazing Amaranth

Tricolor amaranth

AMARANTH DEFINITELY TOOK CENTER STAGE in my family's garden the year I grew a towering cinnamon-orange-flowering variety called 'Hot Biscuits'. I was just a teenager, and I was amazed at the staggering heights it grew to (taller than me!). At the time, though, I had no idea that amaranth was not only edible, but actually a superfood. Its abundant leaves have almost twice the vitamin C of spinach and as much iron, and its seeds are packed with protein.

Today, I grow amaranth in the vegetable garden as well as in big pots on my sunny deck, where we harvest tender leaves from early to midsummer and enjoy the beauty of the flamboyant tassels well into autumn. If we're lucky and the summer is long, we can also harvest mature grains after the first frost.

Amaranth leaves taste similar to spinach, but unlike spinach, which quickly bolts in hot weather, amaranth is both heat and drought tolerant, making it an ideal green for summer production. As a bonus, the seeds have a nice nutty flavor, and are used in hot cereal, breads, and other baked goods.

AN ANCIENT GRAIN FOR A MODERN DIET

Amaranth is a quinoa cousin that originated in Central America, but over the past 400 to 500 years it has spread across the globe, becoming an important food crop for millions of people. The seeds of amaranth are often referred to as and utilized like a grain, but it's not a true grain (grain is the seed of a grass; amaranth is a broadleaf plant, so its seeds are not actually a grain). And speaking of the seeds, they are tiny — about half the size of quinoa seeds — and produced in massive

quantities, with some individual plants yielding up to 100,000 seeds!

As a history enthusiast, I love to grow ancient crops like amaranth, which has been cultivated since at least 6700 BCE. It was an important food crop in the pre-conquest Aztec empire and eventually spread to Europe and Asia. The name "amaranth" derives from the Greek, meaning "life everlasting" and "unfading flower" for its robust growth and prolific reseeding.

VARIED VEGETABLE AMARANTHS

The sizable amaranth family offers about 60 species, which are often tangled together in books and seed catalogs or just lumped under the name "amaranth." The species I've featured here are the ones I think are most important for gardeners to grow. They offer the highest-quality leaves,

THE DETAILS

A.K.A.: *Amaranthus* species

DAYS TO MATURITY: Leaf harvest begins about 45 days from seeding

HAILS FROM: Central America

VARIETIES TO TRY: *Amaranthus dubius, Amaranthus cruentus, Amaranthus tricolor, Amaranthus blitum*

and they're extremely productive and very showy, making them multipurpose plants. With so many species, you'll find quite a range of plant sizes and colors, with heights ranging from 2 to 8 feet.

AMARANTHUS DUBIUS. Known as *doodo* or *dodo* in parts of Africa and the Caribbean, this species is valued for its use as a nutritious cooked green. Plants are fast growing and will reach 3 to 4 feet tall if left uncut. They take well to repeat cutting, though, which results in a continual crop of deep green leaves held on compact, bushy plants. This species tends to be thirstier than *A. cruentus* and requires regular moisture to prevent premature flowering and a decline in leaf quality.

AMARANTHUS CRUENTUS. There are many leafy crops, and even several species of amaranth, that are called *callaloo*, but *A. cruentus* is the starring ingredient in Caribbean and West African cuisine. In South Africa, the green form is called *marog*, and it's used in many traditional dishes. It's also a used for seed production (see page 121).

AMARANTHUS TRICOLOR. This is among the most beautiful of the amaranth species! Thomas Jefferson was so enchanted by it, he brought home seeds from Paris in 1786 to grow at Monticello. He called it "three-colored Amaranth," a description that is also reflected in its Latin name. Generally, the species is divided into two

tasty, showy amaranths

It's not just 'Hot Biscuits' that will make you do a double-take; many amaranth species produce showy tassels in a variety of colors, including blood red, burgundy, orange, salmon, pink, purple, and even lime green. In some species, the flowers grow upright like a living candelabra with fluffy, touchable plumes. With others, the flowers are pendulant, forming long, ropey chains that can cascade to the ground.

There are even species of amaranth where the foliage is showier than the flowers — I'm talking about you, *Amaranthus tricolor!* Often called vegetable amaranth or Joseph's coat, *A. tricolor* yields mounding, poinsettia-like plants with flamboyant red, yellow, green, or orange foliage and tiny, inconspicuous blooms. Because of their ornamental appearance, many species of *Amaranthus,* including *A. tricolor,* are used for edible landscaping and thus can be tucked into flower beds, borders, and pots, with the foliage harvested as needed. The blooms also make excellent and long-lived cut flowers.

Tricolor amaranth

'Hot Biscuits'

Green amaranth

categories: vegetable amaranth and Joseph's coat.

Vegetable amaranth — also known as Chinese spinach, yin choy, and tampala — is a beautiful plant with succulent green, fuschia-red, and purply leaves. Farmers in China grow a number of types of with simple but descriptive names like white leaf, green pointed leaf, round leaf, and red leaf. It's enjoyed in a variety of raw or cooked dishes.

Joseph's coat, on the other hand, is typically grown as an ornamental for flower gardens and has ridiculously showy foliage in a broad range of colors and combinations. This type is still edible, but the plants are not as prolific nor as tender as the less flashy vegetable amaranth.

Under ideal conditions, *A. tricolor* can grow up to 6 feet tall (though 3 to 4 feet is more common). It responds well to pinching, so as the plants grow, don't be shy about removing the terminal buds. This will encourage the plants to branch, which means thicker, bushier plants and a larger harvest.

AMARANTHUS BLITUM. In Greece, wild greens are an important part of the diet, and although *A. blitum* is found natu-ralized in the countryside, it's also semi-domesticated and grown in kitchen gardens for a steady supply of the mild-flavored leaves. Both *A. blitum* and *A. viridis* are known as known as *vlita* (slender ama-ranth) and serve as a popular green for warm or cool cooked salads dressed simply with olive oil, lemon juice, and salt. (My family likes to add some chopped oregano as well for an extra layer of flavor.)

The Greeks prize *A. blitum* for its abil-ity to flourish in the hot summer weather and persist long after spinach has bolted. Because of its spinach similarities, it's also used as a substitute in Greek dishes like spanakopita. The Greeks aren't the only culture to have staked a claim on this leafy vegetable, however: it's also popular in parts of Africa and India, where it is both foraged and cultivated.

Unlike some of the taller, showier ama-ranths, this species grows to just 3 feet and has simple green leaves that may sport a bit of purple. The green flower clusters are also more modest in size and color and produce fewer but larger seeds than most other species of amaranth. As a rule, garden-cultivated *A. blitum* plants will be bigger and higher yielding, offering a better qual-ity of leaf than the wild types.

A HEAT-LOVING GREEN

Unlike most salad greens, which thrive in the cool temperatures of spring and sum-mer, amaranth is a heat lover and shouldn't be planted until the weather is reliably warm in late spring. In Zones 7 to 9, ama-ranth can be direct-seeded once the day-time temperatures are regularly above 70°F (20°C), evening temperatures 60°F (15°C),

and soil temperatures 65°F (18°C). But in Zones 4 to 6, amaranth benefits from a 5- to 6-week head start indoors. Transplant 1 to 2 weeks after the last frost into rich, well-drained soil, in a spot that receives 6 to 8 hours of sun each day.

Amaranth is a bit slow to start grow-ing in the fluctuating temperatures of late spring, so keep on top of weeds in the early days. When the summer heat arrives and the plants begin to grow, they'll easily outcompete most garden weeds. Newly transplanted seedlings benefit from an occasional deep watering; once they're established, amaranth plants are relatively drought tolerant. Amaranth is affected by few diseases, but it can fall prey to cater-pillars, grasshoppers, cucumber beetles, or leaf miners, so keep an eye out for pests and handpick them when possible.

TIPS FOR GROWING GREAT LEAVES

Set seedlings 10 to 12 inches apart or on 10-inch centers. If direct sowing, sprinkle the seeds every 2 inches, eventually thin-ning to the transplanting distance. Be care-ful not to bury the seed too deep; aim for a depth of about ¼ inch. You can also mix the tiny seeds with coarse sand to make sowing easier and more even.

To encourage higher leaf production, give plants a haircut when they are about 10 to 12 inches tall by shearing them back to 6 inches. Just be sure to leave at least two leaves and buds on each plant. Follow this trimming with a dose of liquid fish fertilizer to encourage fresh, well-branched growth.

PACKED WITH NUTRIENTS

Raw, the young leaves are excellent in any fresh dish. The colored varieties do lose their pigments when cooked, but if picked young and eaten raw, they will add a fun pop of color to salads or can serve as a pretty bed for cooked chicken, fish, or meat. They're also used in cooked dishes around the globe and can be incorporated in any dish you'd use spinach for.

Like spinach, beet greens, chard, and sorrel, the leaves of amaranth contain high levels of oxalic acid, which can inhibit the body's absorption of calcium and zinc. If you're prone to kidney stones, you may wish to avoid eating amaranth leaves. Note that young leaves have less oxalic acid than mature leaves, and that boiling or steaming will lower the levels of oxalic acid (though some of the vitamins and minerals will be removed as well).

BUT WAIT! THERE'S MORE: GROWING FOR SEED

In addition to growing amaranth as a spinach substitute, you might want to grow some for its protein-rich seeds. Like the foliage and flowers, the seed color can vary, ranging from cream colored to brown to black. White-seeded varieties are said to have the best-quality grains for cooking. The grains of black- and dark-seeded varieties can be gritty when cooked, but the plants produce very tender leaves. Depending on the species, amaranth grown for its grains will need 100 to 120 days of warm, frost-free weather to reach maturity. You can expect anywhere from a few ounces to 1 pound of seeds per plant, depending on the growing conditions and species. Here are a few species to try.

Purple amaranth

AMARANTHUS CRUENTUS. Also known as African spinach, Mexican grain amaranth, and red amaranth, *A. cruentus* is a multitasking amaranth grown for both its tasty foliage and high seed production. It forms large, narrow plants 4 to 6 feet tall and 1½ feet wide. Leaf color varies from bright green to bronze green to deep red, its thick stems are bright rhubarb red (also edible), and it's topped with burgundy-pink flower spikes in late summer. Outstanding cultivars include 'Hot Biscuits', 'Tower Red', 'Tower Green', and 'Hopi Red Dye' (a plant that was used by people of the Hopi Nation to make their traditional burgundy-purple piki bread).

AMARANTHUS HYPOCHONDRIACUS. This is considered the most productive of the grain amaranths and is the species that became a staple food of the Aztecs. Also called prince's feather or Prince-of-Wales feather, this species has pretty

Amaranthus
cruentus

Amaranthus
hypochondriacus

reddish-green leaves and large, dense flower clusters that yield an ample harvest of seed. The plants will grow to around 5 feet tall and are crowned with the velvety blooms in late summer. Popular varieties include 'Pygmy Torch' and 'Green Thumb', which are (as you might guess) compact plants that grow to just knee-high.

AMARANTHUS CAUDATUS. Commonly known as love-lies-bleeding or tassel flower, this species boasts one of the more curious — and eye-catching — forms of amaranth. The plants themselves grow 3 to 5 feet tall, but when the blood-red flowers emerge, instead of growing up, they hang straight down, cascading as much as 2 feet in length and sometimes touching the ground. Because of the heavy, pendulant blooms, it's best to stake this species as it grows to prevent stem breakage. Try 'Viridis', a green version of the traditional red love-lies-bleeding.

GROWING AND HARVESTING TIPS

Amaranth plants grown for grain production will need a bit more space than those grown for greens. Set seedlings on 15- to 18-inch centers, or direct seed every 6 inches, thinning to 15 to 18 inches as plants become established.

Amaranth is typically wind pollinated and self fertile; each flower spike is composed of hundreds of tiny male and female flowers. As such, it will produce seeds even if grown alone in a pot. Maturation of the seed heads is a gradual process that begins at the bottom of the tassel and moves gradually upward. If the bottom seeds are ripe and ready to fall (test by gently shaking or rubbing the flower head), gather them by simply bending the tassel over a clean bucket or bowl and shaking out the ripe seeds. The head can then be left to continue maturing.

Many gardeners wait to harvest the seed heads until after the first frost, when the plants are on the decline. Shaking the heads over a bowl as they ripen is the easiest and cleanest way to harvest the seed, but sometimes bad weather threatens (frost, storms) and you need to harvest the entire heads at once. In these cases, you can cut the seed heads and hang them upside down in a well-ventilated site; cover them with a paper bag or lay a clean tarp below to catch any seeds that fall. Allow the seed heads to dry for a week or two.

THRESHING AND WINNOWING. Once the heads are mature, thresh them over a clean sheet or into large paper bags to collect all the tiny seeds, using a gloved hand to help separate the seeds from the head (the chaff is rather prickly). Eliminate larger bits of chaff by sifting the seed through a colander or piece of screen.

To separate the seeds from the smallest bits of prickly chaff, place them in a plastic bowl and toss them gently into the air in front of a fan set on low. Adjust the fan speed as needed. As you toss, the lighter chaff will float to the top of the seeds and be blown away, or you can skim it off with a large spoon. Repeat until no chaff remains. Winnowing is a skill that takes practice, and novices should lay a clean sheet or tarp on the ground first so that spilled seeds can quickly be gathered up.

COOKING

Unlike quinoa, the seeds of amaranth have no saponin, the bitter compound that coats quinoa seed and needs to be rinsed off; amaranth seeds can be cooked just as they are. To cook amaranth grains, combine the grains with an equal amount of water and simmer for 10 to 12 minutes. Check the pot occasionally and add more water if the

Amaranthus
caudatus

grains look dry. Besides cooking it simply and serving it like rice, amaranth can also be incorporated into a nutritious breakfast porridge or ground into flour to be baked in muffins or breads.

POPPING AMARANTH

Amaranth is delicious when it's popped like popcorn. Popped amaranth can be added to homemade granola or granola bars, or cereal mixed with yogurt and fruit or just eaten by the spoonful!

To pop amaranth, place a saucepan over medium-high heat. (Unlike with popcorn, there is no need to add oil.) When it's hot, add a scant tablespoon of amaranth grains to the pan; they should start to pop in just a few seconds. Pop a tablespoon at a time, swirling the pan to help the grains pop evenly. Top the pan with a lid or splatter screen to help stop the tiny seeds from popping all over your stove. As each panful is popped, place the grains in a nearby bowl. One tablespoon of amaranth grains will yield 4 to 5 tablespoons of popped grains.

TRY THIS!
Molokhia

THE DETAILS

A.K.A.: Egyptian spinach, jute, jute mallow, *Corchorus olitorius*

DAYS TO MATURITY: 60 days

HAILS FROM: Tropical Africa

VARIETIES TO TRY: None

AT LEAST ONCE A MONTH, my Lebanese mother-in-law cooks molokhia for Sunday lunch. She uses this traditional Middle Eastern green in a thick green stew, dotted with chunks of tender chicken, that is scooped over rice and topped with chopped onions soaked in vinegar. The flavor of molokhia is something like okra with a hint of spinach. It has an okralike texture, too — it becomes mucilaginous when cooked. With molokhia stew, this is a benefit, as it helps to thicken the dish.

My mother-in-law has typically relied on frozen molokhia, or more rarely, dried, for her stew; it's one of the only options for most cooks in North America, as the fresh plant is seldom found at farmers' markets. However, this herbaceous plant is actually very easy to grow. The leaves of fresh molokhia are a treat and can be used in salads or finely chopped for soups, stews, and curries. They're also extremely nutritious, high in iron, calcium, potassium, magnesium, and vitamins C, E, A, and K.

A MEMBER OF THE MALLOWS

Molokhia is a member of the mallow family and originated in Africa. It's been an important ingredient in Egyptian cooking, likely for generations. Eventually, this potherb spread beyond the African border and is now a vegetable enjoyed in many countries. In fact, depending on where you are, you'll find that molokhia spelled in many ways, including "molokheya" and "mulukhiya."

As the common name "jute" implies, this plant is also harvested for its strong stem fibers, which have traditionally been used to make coarse twine or to weave into burlaplike sacks. Perhaps at the end of the growing season, after you have harvested the leaves, you'll want to try to make your own jute twine!

Plants will grow between 3 and 5 feet tall and produce attractive glossy green foliage that resembles mint leaves in shape and size. Molokhia produces pretty yellow flowers, followed by 3-inch-long seedpods that resemble okra pods. (Our kids think they look like rocket ships emerging from the plants.) To save the seed, collect the seeds once the pods have dried. Share with fellow gardeners who want to try growing a Middle Eastern treat.

GIVE IT A WARM START

As with many warm-season crops, molokhia grows best in colder climates when it's started indoors 6 to 8 weeks before the last spring frost. Sow the small seeds thinly in cell packs or small pots, eventually thinning to one plant per pot. When the spring weather has settled, move the plants to a sunny site in the garden, spacing them a foot apart. Before transplanting, dig in some compost or aged manure. Gardeners in Zone 7 and warmer can direct seed. Water weekly if there has been insufficient rain, and feed monthly with a liquid organic fertilizer like fish emulsion.

I grow molokhia in garden beds, but it also grows very well in large containers. Container growing has an added benefit: if frost threatens, potted plants can be brought indoors, stretching the harvest into winter. Just be sure to place the pots near a sunny window.

PINCH TO INCREASE PRODUCTION

Molokhia grows quickly in hot weather, and harvesting can often begin about 4 to 6 weeks from transplanting. When the plants are about a foot and a half tall, begin harvesting, pinching down to a fresh branch or node. This will encourage the plants to send out more side shoots. (More branches means more molokhia!) The thin stems are also edible, so there's no need to trim them off.

Molokhia is a key ingredient in my Lebanese mother-in-law's traditional stew.

Sweet Potato Leaves

I'VE GROWN SWEET POTATOES on and off for years, but I'm embarrassed to admit that until just a few short years ago, I had never eaten the leaves, a popular green vegetable in many parts of the world. To learn more, I turned to Chinese vegetable expert Wendy Kiang-Spray, who points out that sweet potato leaves are a delicious and easy-to-grow alternative to spinach. The plants don't bolt, and the foliage remains mild tasting and tender in hot weather. Plus, they adapt well to a wide variety of growing conditions; in ground gardens, raised beds and container culture.

"Why just look at those fresh and gorgeous sweet potato leaves growing all summer? While you're waiting for your tubers to develop underground, go ahead and cut some leaves from each plant," she says. The vigorous plants respond to regular harvesting by sending out fresh shoots and we are able to pick a big bowl of leaves from our plants every week to 10 days during the summer.

CHOOSING SHOOTS

Despite their name, sweet potatoes are not actually related to potatoes. Rather, they're a member of the morning glory family — as evidenced by their large, heart-shaped leaves. Kiang-Spray says that the leaves of all varieties of sweet potatoes grown for eating are edible, but she notes that there are some variations in taste. The ornamental sweet potatoes often grown in non-edible container gardens are not suited to eating.

In Kiang-Spray's garden, she grows a family heirloom that produces white tubers, but it's not the tubers she's after. "The tubers from our variety are not as delicious as other varieties of sweet potato, but the nutritious leaves are more mild and tender," she says. In my region, I found a small specialty nursery that offers around a dozen varieties of short season sweet potatoes, including several which have tender, tasty foliage.

STARTING FROM SLIPS

Sweet potatoes are typically grown from slips, 5- to 6-inch shoots that grow from the tuber. You can grow your own slips from a sweet potato or you can buy them in nurseries or from specialty catalogs in early spring. Another option is to buy bundles of fresh sweet potato greens at the Asian supermarket in early spring and root those shoots to make your own slips. That way, you know you're getting a variety that yields high-quality greens.

BRING ON THE HEAT

Sweet potatoes love heat, so cool-climate gardeners should consider preheating their soil by laying black plastic on top of garden beds for 2 weeks before planting. This will minimize transplant shock. Building hills of soil for the plants also helps; the soil will warm up more quickly this way and stay warmer through the summer. Be sure to pick a sunny site and dig in organic matter like compost or rotted manure to enrich the soil.

Sweet
potato
leaves

As the vines grow, they'll form a natural mulch on the soil surface, discouraging weeds and helping to retain soil moisture. That said, the highest-quality leaves (and tubers) come from plants that are regularly irrigated. Give them 1 to 2 inches of water per week if there has been no deep rain.

You can also grow a leafy crop of sweet potato greens in a large pot — at least 15 inches in diameter — filled with a mixture of potting soil and compost. Plant one slip per pot, supplement with a liquid organic fertilizer every month, and water often.

As the plants grow, harvest handfuls of the delicately flavored leaves from the plants. If you wish to encourage tuber production, don't take too much from any one plant. Instead, spread the harvest among a number of plants.

COOK AND ENJOY

My first foray into eating sweet potato greens was simple, but memorable. I boiled the leaves for 2 to 3 minutes, then drained and topped them with a drizzle of olive oil, salt, and a pinch of garlic powder. Delicious! But there are many other ways to enjoy this easy-to-grow green. In Chinese and South American cuisine, Wendy Kiang-Spray says that sweet potato greens are typically eaten stir-fried, boiled, or sautéed. She says that her mom boils the leaves until wilted and then tops them with flash-fried chopped garlic and oyster sauce.

THE DETAILS

A.K.A.: *Ipomoea batatas*

DAYS TO MATURITY: 60 days from transplanting slips

HAILS FROM: Central to South America

VARIETIES TO TRY: 'Korean Purple', 'Tainung 65', 'Ringseng Red'

TRY THIS!
Tasty Tatsoi

THE DETAILS
A.K.A.: Spoon mustard, *Brassica rapa* var. *rosularis*

DAYS TO MATURITY: 21 days for baby greens, 45 days for full-size heads

HAILS FROM: China

VARIETIES TO TRY: Green tatsoi, red tatsoi

IN MY WINTER COLD FRAMES, tatsoi is a cold-season superstar, shrugging off frigid temperatures and giving us an ample harvest of crunchy leaves from November through March. I love to add the raw leaves to mixed greens salads, but the young, whole plants are also tasty when lightly stir-fried with other vegetables and aromatics like ginger and garlic.

Tatsoi is a nonheading member of the mustard family that forms low-growing rosettes of deep green, spoon-shaped leaves. The texture of the leaf is similar to that of spinach, but the flavor carries a hint of mustard. It's still considered mild on the flavor spectrum, however, which is why it's such a popular ingredient in bagged baby greens.

one more to try
'Yukina Savoy' Chinese cabbage is a tatsoi-like green that can also be used interchangeably with spinach. It's very fast growing and forms pretty, upright rosettes of deep green, crinkly leaves. See page 143 for more information.

EASY AND SPEEDY
When I first grew tatsoi, it was hard to source the seed. Happily, with the increase in fall and winter vegetable gardening, it's becoming quite popular and is now found in seed catalogs across North America and the United Kingdom. It's a very easy, super speedy crop to grow. Baby plants are ready just 3 to 4 weeks from seeding.

Tatsoi is best direct-seeded in garden beds, cold frames, or containers. Like many hardy greens, it thrives in the cool temperatures and increased moisture of spring and fall, but we also grow it in summer by sowing the seed in the partial shade beneath the A-frame trellises and tepees that support vining crops.

For the highest-quality and quickest crop, enrich the soil with compost or aged manure before planting. We succession plant every 3 weeks to be sure we're never without this useful spinach substitute. Spring-sown tatsoi can be susceptible to bolting when grown in the open garden, so wait until after the last frost to seed in unprotected garden beds. If you're planting in the shelter of cold frames or beneath a mini hoop tunnel, you can sow seed 6 to 8 weeks before the last expected frost.

Keep a watch for flea beetles, which also love to munch on this green. To minimize damage, practice crop rotation and cover the plants with row cover or insect barrier after seeding.

The harvest of baby leaves can begin about 3 weeks from sowing. Remove the outer leaves and allow the center of the plant to continue growing. It will form rosettes 8 to 10 inches across if left to mature. Young plants can be harvested whole for stir-frying.

TRY THIS!
New Zealand Spinach

IF I TOLD YOU THAT THERE WAS a leafy green vegetable that thrives in the heat of summer, is drought tolerant, and not bothered by diseases or pests like flea beetles, leaf miners, and aphids, you'd want to grow it in your garden, wouldn't you? Me too! So, let me introduce you to New Zealand spinach.

It is not really a spinach relative, but it is often compared to spinach because of its similarly mild flavor and because of how the two greens are prepared in the kitchen. In North America, the United Kingdom, and Europe, New Zealand spinach is grown as a summer green, thriving when spinach and most other salad and cooking greens have succumbed to the heat.

"Down Under," this plant is a perennial known as warrigal greens, and according to the diary of Joseph Banks, the botanist on board the *Endeavour*, Captain James Cook and his crew dined on it to prevent scurvy. It is high in vitamins A and C (just in case you're also worried about scurvy).

A GORGEOUS GREEN FROM DOWN UNDER

The low-spreading form, brilliant green color, and small yellow blooms of New Zealand spinach make this a very ornamental plant. If you don't have a vegetable garden (or much space), try using it for edible landscaping — perhaps along the front of a perennial bed as an edging plant or ground cover. Expect it to grow 1 to

New Zealand spinach

Because initial growth is slow, New Zealand spinach can be interplanted with a quick-growing early crop like spring beets, radishes, carrots, turnips, or various cool-season greens.

THE DETAILS

A.K.A.: Summer spinach, perennial spinach, ever-bearing spinach, Cook's cabbage, *Tetragonia tetragonoides*

DAYS TO MATURITY: 50 days

HAILS FROM: South Pacific, South America, coastal regions of China and Japan

VARIETIES TO TRY: None

1½ feet tall. No garden? No problem! Plant the seedlings in pots or planters on a deck or patio. Just remember that it's a sprawling plant and appreciates ample root room, so choose pots at least 15 inches in diameter and ensure there is good drainage.

The triangular, almost diamond-shaped leaves of New Zealand spinach are fleshy and covered in tiny silvery hairs, which are especially pretty on the new growth. The leaves are thicker and meatier than spinach, and they don't wilt quickly after harvest.

PERENNIAL OR NOT?

Don't let the term "perennial" in its common name fool you — it's not perennial in much of North America. In warm regions, like Florida, it can be invasive, but in my Zone 5 garden it's an annual crop that we enjoy from late June through late September. It can reseed, though, so don't be surprised if you see New Zealand spinach babies popping up the following spring.

Like common spinach, New Zealand spinach is easy to grow, productive, and extremely versatile in the kitchen. Just when our spinach crop begins to bolt with the arrival of early summer, the New Zealand spinach is ready to take its place.

Another similarity between spinach and New Zealand spinach is that both are high in oxalates, which can cause kidney stones in those who are susceptible. We eat this as a cooked green, but first we blanch the leaves to remove some of the oxalic acid. That said, I know many gardeners who like to eat New Zealand spinach raw in salads and don't mind the bitter bite of the uncooked leaves.

New Zealand spinach is a heat lover and, in northern regions, grows best in a sunny site. Southern gardeners, on the other hand, should seek a partially shaded spot or one that offers a bit of afternoon respite from the sun. As to how many plants you will need, keep in mind that the plants are very productive, and a handful should be sufficient for a family of four. If you plan on freezing the greens for winter use, plant an additional five or six plants.

STUBBORN TO GERMINATE, BUT EASY EVER AFTER

In the garden, New Zealand spinach is a "hands-off" crop and needs little coddling. Yet before it reaches that stage, you must germinate the seeds, and this is where things can get tricky. Seed catalogs often recommend soaking the seeds for 24 hours to hasten germination, but I've also had success gently scoring them with a nail file to damage the seed coat.

It's important to note that the "seeds" (which, coincidentally, are actually tiny fruits that each contain up to 10 seeds) don't germinate at the same rate; some may pop up after 10 days, while others can take 3 weeks to emerge, so be patient. Once the young plants have seven or eight true leaves, they can be hardened off and transplanted into the garden, around 3 to 4 weeks after germination.

New Zealand spinach does fine in average, well-drained soil but grows best in beds that have been amended with 2 to 3 inches of compost or aged manure. Ample organic matter will encourage plenty of tender tip growth, the part of the plant you want to eat. I also dig in some alfalfa meal and kelp meal. Space plants 12 inches to 18 inches apart, or on 18-inch centers. Because of their tendency to sprawl, they'll cover more horizontal space than vertical space. Happily, this dense, low habit also discourages weed growth.

This is a drought-tolerant crop, but the best quality and flavor come from plants that have been irrigated. Therefore, supply about an inch of water per week if Mother Nature hasn't been accommodating. It's also beneficial to give the plants a dose of fish emulsion or similar organic, high-nitrogen fertilizer, every month or so.

PICKING SHOOTS

The harvest will begin in earnest around 2 months after germination, when the plants are about a foot tall. The edible part — or at least the best-quality eating — comes from the shoot tips. To harvest, pinch off 3 to 4 inches of the tender growing tips. This will stimulate side-shoot production and thicken up the plants, ensuring many more harvests to come. You'll want to harvest often — at least every week to 10 days to keep leaf quality and shoot production high. Avoid picking the older leaves, which are less palatable, slightly bitter, and unpleasantly fibrous.

I like to harvest the shoots just before I need them, but they can also be picked and stored in a plastic baggie in the refrigerator, where they will retain their freshness for up to a week.

Keep the harvest going into fall and even winter by digging up a few New Zealand spinach plants and bringing them indoors in late summer. Give them plenty of light and harvest often to encourage production.

New Zealand spinach

Orach

TRY THIS!
Ornamental Orach

THE FIRST TIME I SAW ORACH, it wasn't growing in a vegetable garden — it was part of a demonstration garden that showcased plants for edible landscaping. Boy, did it stand out! I was immediately taken with the bold purple-burgundy foliage and by the fact that the plants were almost 4 feet tall. The following spring, I added packets of 'Aurora' and 'Ruby Red' orach to my seed order.

Orach is an ancient crop, often described as spinach's sexier cousin. (They're both part of the amaranth family, along with quinoa, beets, and Swiss chard.) Unlike spinach, though, orach is quite bolt resistant, providing nutritious leaves well into summer.

A COLORFUL, CITRUSY SPINACH COUSIN

Orach comes in some pretty bold colors! Depending on the variety, foliage can range from light to dark green, pink to red, burgundy to purple, and yellow to gold. One of the most popular is 'Aurora', an outstanding rainbow strain that offers leaves in hues of lime green, red, carmine, pink, green, gold, and purple.

In general, orach has a mild citrus taste, but different colors offer slightly different variations of flavor. Red leaves have the most zing, green plants have a milder taste, and the gold varieties have the sweetest leaves. Orach is a popular green to add to sorrel salads, because it helps balance the intense sourness of sorrel.

Like most orach lovers, I appreciate the colors, but I also love its form: upright and narrow, almost columnar. The plants can grow very tall — 6 feet or more (though in my garden, they usually top out around 3 to 3½ feet) — but just 1 to 1½ feet wide, allowing you to cram quite a few plants into a garden bed.

GROW GREAT ORACH

Orach is tolerant of many soils, but it will produce the highest-quality crop and resist bolting for a longer period of time if it is given decent soil amended with compost or aged manure. Full sun is best for northern gardeners, but those in warmer climates might want to plant orach in partial or afternoon shade to discourage early bolting.

The seed germinates in cool temperatures (50 to 60°F/10 to 15°C) and can be direct-seeded in early spring, about 2 to 3 weeks before the last expected frost, or started indoors in 4-inch pots or cell packs. If direct seeding, space seed every 2 inches and expect germination to take 1 to 2 weeks. Keep the seedbed moist until you see the tiny shoots. Orach started indoors can be hardened off and moved to the garden after 3 to 4 weeks of growth. Space seedlings at least a foot apart.

As your direct-seeded (or self-seeded) orach seedlings grow, thin them to a foot apart (or 18 inches, if you want to encourage very large plants). I let the young plants grow to 6 inches tall before thinning them; these tender young greens and shoots can be eaten raw or lightly sautéed.

Mulch young plants with shredded leaves or straw to help conserve soil moisture. Orach is moderately drought tolerant, but eating quality will be higher in plants that aren't water stressed.

HARVEST AT EVERY STAGE

Orach can be harvested at virtually any stage — from tiny microgreens to mature flowering plants — but as with most greens, the best quality comes from immature plants. Once the plants are bigger than 18 inches, you can continue to harvest greens, but stick to the youngest leaves at the top of the plant.

As the plants switch from vegetative growth to flowering, you can pull them out and succession plant with another crop. But if you have the space, allow some plants to flower. The large flower spikes remind me of quinoa and are incredibly ornamental. Plus, they attract pollinators and beneficial insects like bees and hoverflies.

We like to eat orach as a young salad crop, but it can also be cooked like spinach. The more colorful varieties will bleed color into whatever you're cooking, which can make risotto, plain rice, and even smoothies rather colorful (and maybe encourage the kids to eat up?).

SAVE SEEDS OR LET THEM SELF-SOW

If you wish to save seeds, cut the flower heads when they begin to turn yellow, bringing them indoors to continue drying. I find it helpful to hang them in large paper bags to catch any seed that threatens to fall. The small black seeds are contained in flat, circular papery husks with one seed per husk. You can rub the husks to remove all the seeds, but you can also just leave the husks on and plant them, too. No need for time-consuming winnowing of the seed! You may find that when you open a packet of orach seed, the seeds are still in their husks.

Orach can be an aggressive self-sower, so remove the flower heads before the seeds mature if you don't wish to be thinning a carpet of seedlings the next spring. That said, leaving the flower heads in the garden will thrill the birds, who like to feast on the seeds. Your choice!

THE DETAILS

A.K.A.: Mountain spinach, French spinach, giant lamb's quarters, *Atriplex hortensis*

DAYS TO MATURITY: 45–60 days

HAILS FROM: Europe and western Asia (naturalized in North America)

VARIETIES TO TRY: 'Aurora', 'Ruby Red'

TRY THIS!
Malabar Spinach

THE DETAILS

A.K.A.: Indian spinach, Ceylon spinach, vining spinach, *saan choy, mong toi, Basella alba, B. rubra*

DAYS TO MATURITY: 70 days

HAILS FROM: India

VARIETIES TO TRY: None

LIKE NEW ZEALAND SPINACH, Malabar spinach basks in the summer heat, supplying leafy greens throughout July, August, and September. But this is where the comparison ends. As a vining plant, Malabar spinach has a completely different form, and it also differs in texture. The mature leaves are thick and fleshy, with a mucilaginous texture. I tend to use only the young, less slimy leaves for salads and uncooked dishes — the peppery flavor is sometimes compared to arugula. Like okra (another slimy veggie!), the mature leaves are good at thickening up soups, gumbo, sauces, and stews.

This is a popular green in much of Asia, as well as Africa, and is becoming quite common in both North and South America. It's a nutritional powerhouse, having amounts of vitamin A, iron, and calcium similar to those of spinach, but with significantly more vitamin C. In addition to being nutritious, the red form, *Basella rubra*, is very attractive; its vibrant reddish purple stems add a pop of color to the garden and the salad bowl. The white species is also a pretty plant, and, like the red type, has large, glossy, heart-shaped leaves. When cooked, both kinds have a flavor that is similar to spinach.

GET GROWING INDOORS

In most regions of North America, you'll need to start this plant indoors, 6 to 7 weeks before the last expected frost. Gardeners in Zone 7 or warmer can direct seed a few weeks after the last spring frost, but starting seeds indoors will cut down on the waiting time from seed to harvest. The seeds, which are the size and color of black peppercorns, should be soaked overnight before planting or scarified with a nail file to hasten germination.

Germination is helped by warm temperatures. If possible, place the just-seeded pots or trays on a heat mat or in a part of your house where the temperature is at least 70°F (21°C). That said, germination will still be slow — 2 to 3 weeks or longer. In my cool basement (60 to 65°F/15 to 18°C), where my seed-starting setup is located, germination can take as long as 4 weeks.

When the plants are hardened off and the risk of frost has passed, get the garden bed or containers ready. Malabar spinach likes full sun and a rich, moist soil, so dig

in 2 to 3 inches of compost or aged manure. Be sure your vertical supports are in place! Place pots against a chain-link fence, trellis, or netting, or in a pinch, use a tomato cage to support the plant. In the garden, space plants at least a foot apart.

WARM WEATHER = RAPID GROWTH

As with many tropical plants, Malabar spinach will grow slowly until the temperature climbs into the 80s on a regular basis. At that point, stand back! The plants will go into high gear, quickly scaling their supports. In southern climates, plants can be grown in shade or partial shade. They will grow larger leaves this way, but their growth rate will slow.

In tropical areas like its native habitat of southern India and Indonesia, the vines of Malabar spinach can grow 12 feet or more. In North American gardens, they will be shorter (6 to 10 feet), but still very striking. Not sure how much to grow? One or two plants should be enough for a family of four.

Plants that aren't given sufficient water will quickly turn to flower and seed production, which makes the leaves less palatable. To meet the water needs of Malabar spinach, you'll probably need to irrigate on a regular basis. I usually end up watering once or twice a week, but we have had wet summers where I watered far less. A soaker hose is an easy way to reduce water waste. Besides the watering, the plants are low maintenance and not typically bothered by common pests, although in the interest of full disclosure, I've caught the slugs occasionally taking a nibble (but what *don't* they eat?).

The dark purple berries add to the ornamental aspect of this plant and are nontoxic. I've heard they make a good jam, but I've yet to try that. We do use them as a natural dye, and the kids have used them as body paint — be warned they do stain clothing (not that the kids seem to care). The seeds are in these berries, and you can save them by allowing the berries to dry on the vines, or pick them and dry them indoors.

PICK 'EM YOUNG FOR RAW EATING

If you want raw greens for salads, wraps, sandwiches, smoothies, and burgers, pick the leaves while still immature. Once they've reached their full size, they're fleshy and mucilaginous, which, for many people, is less palatable raw. The youngest, most tender leaves will be at the tops of the vines. Snip the shoots and add them whole to lasagna, stir-fries, quiche, curry, or pastas. As with many of the other greens I've discussed, Malabar spinach has high levels of oxalic acid, so avoid overindulging if you're susceptible to kidney stones.

Malabar spinach can be grown from seed, but you can also take stem or stem tip cuttings, which root quickly and easily.

TRY THIS!
Hardy Hablitzia

HABLITZIA TAMNOIDES **IS A** recent addition to my garden, thanks to Telsing Andrews of Aster Lane Edibles in Ontario, Canada, a small nursery that specializes in ornamental, perennial, and unique edibles. A few weeks after she sang the praises of this productive perennial crop on my radio show, an envelope of hablitzia seeds arrived in my mailbox. I sowed the seeds, and before long, the young plants were tucked in a partially shaded corner in my backyard. Like most perennial plants, hablitzia takes a year or two to establish, but when settled in, the vigorous plants provide a dual harvest of tender spring shoots followed by several months of mild spinachlike greens.

Hablitzia is a member of the sizable amaranth family and is related to spinach as well as orach, chard, and beets. There are a few common names for this unusual climber — spinach vine, climbing spinach, Caucasian spinach — but it seems that it's most often called by its Latin name to distinguish it from other climbing spinachlike plants (such as Malabar spinach). The name "Caucasian spinach" is a nod to its lineage, which can be traced to the Caucasus region that joins Europe and Asia. In its native habitat, hablitzia is an herbaceous vine that grows in the woodlands and beside streams and rivers and scrambles over the rocks in the Caucasus Mountains.

Hablitiza has been grown as a food crop in Scandinavia (attesting to its extreme cold hardiness!) and the United Kingdom, but until recently, it's been fairly unknown in North America. Plant collectors like Stephen Barstow and perennial food gardeners like Eric Toensmeier are shining a spotlight on this underused crop, so the seeds are becoming easier to source.

A SHADY CHARACTER

Most gardeners will grow hablitzia from seed, although you can also take root divisions if you're lucky to have a friend with a mature plant. Starting the seed isn't difficult, but it's a bit trickier than sowing annual vegetable seeds like those of tomatoes. For example, hablitzia germinates best at low temperatures — just above freezing — a trait that likely comes from its native habitat, where the growing season is short and winters are cold. As recommended by Stephen Barstow in his book, *Around the World in 80 Plants*, I sowed my seed in 4-inch pots, slipped them in plastic bags, and placed them in the fridge. After 2 weeks, I noticed that tiny green shoots had emerged, and I quickly moved the pots beneath the grow lights in my cool basement.

Because hablitiza is a perennial plant, put a bit of extra care into picking a good site for it. In its natural environment, it grows in the dappled shade of the forest, often near running water. Therefore, a spot with full sun may not be ideal, unless the soil is naturally moist. If bright sunshine is your only option, dig in plenty of organic matter before you plant, to boost the water-holding capacity of the soil.

Ideally, seek out a site with partial shade, such as beneath deciduous trees. As with many edible plants, those that are grown in partial shade will yield slightly later than those grown in full sun. If you want to be sneaky and get the longest possible harvest, consider planting hablitiza in both sun and partial shade.

Irrigate weekly during the first season, unless there has been regular, soaking rain. Hablitzia doesn't want to have wet feet, but soil that is too dry will quickly kill it. In subsequent years, water occasionally in summer or during drought. It's also a good idea to mulch the plants with shredded leaves or another natural material to preserve soil moisture.

Halblitizia may be a rambunctious perennial vine, but it's not out to take over your entire garden. In fact, the shoots die back to the ground each autumn and reemerge the following spring.

HARVEST EARLY

Established hablitzia forms dense clumps that emerge very early in the season. Look for those first shoots, which can — and should! — be harvested when they're 2 to 4 inches long. They're very pretty; the green rosettes are tinged with pink under the leaves and on the stems. Mature plants will offer repeated harvests of tender shoots over a period of several weeks. Eat them either raw or cooked.

After harvesting two or three crops, allow the shoots to develop into the ridiculously fast-growing vines. How fast? Depending on their growing conditions, they can reach heights of 8 feet or more in mere weeks! At this point, the harvest will switch from shoots to the mild-tasting heart-shaped leaves. These can also be eaten raw as a green, or treated like spinach in your favorite cooked dishes.

The new leaves are the best eating and quite attractive — bright green and heart-shaped. As they mature, they become more arrow-shaped, and soon masses of tiny green flowers emerge. It's a good idea to provide some type of structure for the plants to climb. They're not robust climbers, but if you tuck them at the base of deciduous trees, they'll eventually find their way up the trunk, reaching lengths of 6 to 10 feet. They can also be trellised against a wall or fence or grown up a tepee structure, like those used for pole beans.

THE DETAILS

A.K.A.: Spinach vine, climbing spinach, Caucasian spinach, *Hablitzia tamnoides*

DAYS TO MATURITY: Perennial crop, approximately Zones 4 to 9, perhaps colder; expect to begin harvesting 1–2 years after planting

HAILS FROM: Caucasus Mountains

VARIETIES TO TRY: None

like cabbage?

try these!

'Green Seoul'
Chinese cabbage

Komatsuna

'Hon Tsai Tai'

'Yukina Savoy'

I've always loved cabbage; even as a young child, I would grab handfuls of just-sliced cabbage my mother was prepping for coleslaw. The sweet flavor and big crunch was so appealing. Even today, cabbage is a favorite in our garden. We plant several crops a year: in spring for an early-summer harvest, and again in midsummer for fall and winter harvesting.

For most people, cabbage is a roundheaded green vegetable. But flip through any seed catalog and you'll quickly see that there are many shapes, sizes, and colors — from cone-headed heirlooms to barrel-shaped Chinese cabbages. I'm very fond of the many varieties of Chinese cabbages, both heading and nonheading, as well as the cabbagelike Asian green komatsuna (which is actually in the turnip family).

TRY THIS!
Chinese Cabbage

WHEN IT COMES TO CHINESE CABBAGE, there is quite a tangle of different types, but I like to divide them into two main groups: heading and nonheading. Heading types include the barrel-shaped varieties like 'Blues' as well as the tall, cylindrical varieties like 'Green Rocket'. The nonheading types form loose rosettes of leafy greens and include varieties like 'Yukina Savoy' and 'Green Seoul'.

Chinese cabbages are very decorative plants, with leaves that can be wide or narrow, smooth or frilly, upright or spreading. Tuck seedlings in ornamental gardens between perennials and bedding plants, or grow them in large pots. The nonheading types are usually very fast to mature and take well to container culture.

Some varieties have a mild, almost sweet flavor, while others have more of a mustardy kick. Don't be afraid to experiment with the complex and extensive range of greens available through seed catalogs; most are easy to grow and thrive with little care.

KEEP IT COOL, MOIST, AND RICH

Chinese cabbages grow best in cool weather. I do plant a few varieties beneath a mini hoop tunnel in early spring, but my main crop comes from my mid- to late-summer plantings, which mature in the cool temperatures and ample moisture of autumn. Quick-growing loose-head or flowering types like 'Hon Tsai Tai' or 'Yukina Savoy' will yield a reliable spring crop, but many Chinese cabbages will bolt if exposed to a sudden shift from cold to hot temperatures,

'Green Seoul'
Chinese cabbage

so plan to harvest before the weather transitions from spring to summer.

These plants aren't too fussy about soil type, but they do want plenty of organic matter. Dig in several inches of rotted manure or compost before planting. I also incorporate a slow-release balanced organic granular fertilizer at planting time.

Start seeds indoors 6 weeks before your last expected frost date, earlier if you intend to plant them beneath a mini hoop tunnel. Once the risk of frost has passed, move the hardened-off seedlings into the garden. Space compact cultivars a foot apart and larger heading types up to 18 inches apart.

You can also direct seed 1 to 2 weeks before the last expected frost date, but I find the young plants are very attractive to slugs; it's much easier to give them a head start indoors. For fall crops, sow additional seed indoors under your grow lights and set out the fresh transplants in midsummer.

As the plants grow, water regularly, giving at least 2 inches of water per week. A 3-inch layer of straw or shredded leaves can be applied to the soil surface to cut down on watering. Also, keep an eye out for pests like cabbageworms. Because my garden is *plagued* by cabbageworms, I protect the bed with a mini hoop tunnel covered

THE DETAILS

A.K.A.: Pe-tsai, napa cabbage, *Brassica rapa* var. *pekinensis*, *B. rapa* var. *chinensis*

DAYS TO MATURITY: Varies by cultivar

HAILS FROM: China

VARIETIES TO TRY: 'Minuet', 'Blues', 'Little Jade', 'Yukina Savoy', 'Green Seoul', 'Maruba Santoh'

'Yukina Savoy'

in a lightweight row cover as soon as the seedlings are planted in spring. This allows air, sun, and water to pass but prevents the white cabbage butterflies from laying their eggs on my seedlings.

Harvest cabbage and heading types of Chinese cabbage when they are firm and approaching their suggested days to maturity. For nonheading Chinese cabbage, you can harvest when young for a baby crop or allow the plants to grow to their mature size.

HEADING TYPES TO TRY

'MINUET' (50 days). This hardy little hybrid forms compact, 9-inch-tall and 6- to 7-inch-wide heads with bright green leaves and large white stems. The flavor is mild and sweet, and the plants are slow to bolt but quick to mature. Seedlings can be transplanted 4 to 6 weeks before the last spring frost in a mini hoop tunnel, or planted in late summer for a tender fall crop.

'BLUES' (55–60 days). This is a popular, reliable Japanese variety that forms dense heads that can weigh up to 4 pounds! The outer foliage is medium green, with light green inner leaves, and the wide mid-ribs are bright white. It is bolt resistant and can be grown for a spring or fall crop. We like to slice the raw leaves into bite-size pieces and drizzle them with a sweet dressing made from soy sauce, sesame oil, sugar, and rice vinegar for a delicious Asian salad.

'LITTLE JADE' (60 days). The compact, firm heads of 'Little Jade' are the perfect size for one family meal. They grow about 8 inches tall and 4 inches wide, with an attractive vase shape. The plants are disease resistant and thrive in the cool weather of spring or fall.

NONHEADING TYPES TO TRY

'YUKINA SAVOY' (25 days baby, 45 days mature). I adore tatsoi and grow it practically year-round, so the thought of a similar, perhaps more productive, crop made me order this seed immediately. We found it to be just as described: the plants formed attractive, deep green rosettes of crinkly, savoyed leaves and grew up to a foot tall. Like tatsoi, it thrives in our cold frames, but we also grow it in the open garden in spring and fall. The baby leaves make high-quality salads, and the mature foliage can be used to replace cabbage in stir-fries and soups.

'GREEN SEOUL' (60–70 days). This variety of Chinese cabbage is very popular in Korea, where it is used to make kimchi. It forms large, loose clusters of lime green leaves, which contrast nicely against the deep green leaves of tatsoi, spinach, or 'Yukina Savoy'. We like the immature leaves in salads; you can also pick the whole plants young by slicing them off at soil level, then cut them in half or quarters, and toss them in a stir-fry.

'MARUBA SANTOH' (35–40 days). This is a veggie with much to recommend it: large, rounded leaves with a mild mustardy flavor; crisp white stems; small broccoli-like flower buds; and pretty, edible blossoms. Like many other Asian greens, 'Maruba Santoh' is quick to grow, ready in just over a month from direct seeding. It's also cold tolerant and can be seeded in a cold frame in early autumn for a late-fall or winter crop; alternatively, you can simply protect a bed of established plants with a mini hoop tunnel in late autumn and harvest into winter. It is susceptible to flea beetles, though, so plant in mid to late spring, after the first population has waned.

Yu Choy Sum

TRY THIS!
Yu Choy Sum

THE DETAILS

A.K.A.: Choy sum, Chinese flowering cabbage, *Brassica rapa* var. *parachinensis*

DAYS TO MATURITY: Varies by cultivar

HAILS FROM: China

VARIETIES TO TRY: 'Early Green', 'Hon Tsai Tai', 'Gunsho'

YU CHOY SUM IS A flowering brassica, sometimes called Chinese flowering cabbage, with edible leaves, stems, and flower buds — perfect for stir-fries through the season! It's both easy and quick to grow, and doesn't take up much space, making it a good choice for urban gardens. Unlike most leafy crops, it's harvested after the plants have bolted (begun to produce flower stalks).

Yu choy sum loses its quality quickly after harvesting, making commercially grown crops both expensive and often of low quality. But it's perfect for gardeners who can take this tasty crop from garden to table in mere minutes!

Grow it in spring or autumn, succession planting small crops every few weeks. This will yield the longest and highest-quality crop of yu choy sum. Harvesting begins when the flower stalks emerge and the yellow blooms open. Slice the stalks, leaving some leaves attached — these are delicious, too! Once the initial center stalk has been harvested, smaller side shoots will develop.

'EARLY GREEN' (35–40 days). This is a super speedy crop that is ready just 4 to 5 weeks from sowing. Slice the immature plants off at soil level — when they're 6 or 7 inches tall — and stir-fry them whole. The plants can be eaten as a stem and leaf crop (yu choy) or when it has produced its flower buds (yu choy sum).

'HON TSAI TAI' (35–40 days). This outstanding open-pollinated green has several names, but hon tsai tai and kosaitai are the most common. The plants are striking, with burgundy-purple stems and deep green leaves that have a mild mustard tang. If harvesting as a yu choy sum crop, the small flower clusters will add to the beauty of the finished dish.

'GUNSHO' (40 days). This hybrid variety offers a reliable crop of bright green stems, leaves, and flower buds. Pick when the stems are about pencil thickness or just as the flower buds emerge. If you leave a stub when harvesting, the plants will often regrow for a cut-and-come-again crop.

'Gunsho'

'Hon Tsai Tai'

Komatsuna

THE DETAILS

A.K.A.: Japanese mustard spinach, *Brassica rapa* var. *perviridis*

DAYS TO MATURITY: 35–45 days

HAILS FROM: Eurasia

VARIETIES TO TRY: 'Torasan', 'Summerfest', 'Carlton', 'Tendergreen', red komatsuna

KOMATSUNA IS AN ASIAN GREEN with an identity crisis. It's a member of the turnip family, but it tastes like cabbage and has overtones of mustard. So where does it belong? It's up to you! I use the large paddle-shaped leaves as a cabbage substitute when making cabbage rolls, stir-fries, or braises. It's also much quicker than heading cabbage to grow from seed to harvest and can even handle the frigid temperatures of winter when grown in a cold frame.

In Japan, Korea, and Taiwan, komatsuna is extremely popular and readily available at fresh markets. In North America, it's less well known. I did see it gracing a few stalls under the name "spinach mustard" at my local farmers' market last autumn, though, so perhaps it will become common here, too. Fully grown komatsuna will be ready about 6 weeks from seeding, but it can be harvested at any stage, from microgreen to mature plant. Even the broccoli-like flower buds and yellow blooms are edible!

FINE FOR PARTIAL SHADE

Komatsuna is grown in much the same way as tatsoi and mizuna. You can give it a head start indoors, but it takes well to direct seeding and can be sown in early spring, about 2 to 3 weeks before the last expected frost. It will grow best if planted in full sun, but if you need to save your sunniest sites for heat lovers like tomatoes and peppers, rest assured that komatsuna will do just fine in partial shade. In fact, a little shade will help delay bolting, especially in Zone 6 and warmer. Enrich the soil with some compost or aged manure and sow the seeds 1 inch apart. These should be thinned a few weeks later to 6 inches for a harvest of baby plants, or 12 inches to allow for full-grown giants.

FALL PLANTS ARE BEST

Our spring crop never grows as large as our fall komatsuna. Once the weather heats up, the early planting soon bolts, so we pull it and replace it with a succession crop. Autumn-grown komatsuna offers the largest, best-tasting leaves and is bothered by fewer pests.

As the weather cools, we cover the bed of komatsuna with a mini hoop tunnel to shelter the crop. We also plant it in cold frames for easy winter harvesting. Like kale, the flavor sweetens with repeated frost. The best flavor and quality come from a steady supply of moisture, so water weekly if there has been no rain, and mulch with straw.

I find komatsuna to be moderately slug and snail resistant. My guess is that the thicker leaves are less attractive to them than the nearby napa cabbages and lettuce. It can be prone to flea beetles, so cover with a row cover in spring if these are an annual problem in your garden.

CUTTING KOMATSUNA

Our spring-grown komatsuna crop is for salads and quick stir-fries. We pick individual leaves or cut the entire plants at ground level. They can be treated as a cut-and-come-again crop, but they don't respond as well to this as other greens do, and they tend to be slow to regrow.

Large, fall-grown komatsuna is great for making cabbage rolls and any other recipe that calls for regular cabbage, but I also love to use the big leaves for wraps. Just fill them with your favorite mixture of vegetables or meat and enjoy. In Asia, komatsuna is also pickled or fermented.

Senposai

sensational senposai

If you like cabbage, you're going to love senposai, a Japanese cross of cabbage and komatsuna. Like komatsuna, senposai is nonheading; it forms wide rosettes of large, flat, cabbagelike leaves (think Ping-Pong paddle). It's also quick growing and more heat tolerant than cabbage, making it a good choice for the summer garden. The flavor is similar to cabbage: mild and sweet. Like komatsuna, the leaves of senposai are great for cabbage rolls — they don't tear as easily as cabbage leaves do.

WHY GROW ORDINARY CABBAGE?

We love the variety and flavors offered by the many types of Asian greens, but we also appreciate traditional cabbages, especially if they have unconventional shapes and colors.

'JANUARY KING' (160–200 days). Aptly named, this heirloom cabbage is a cold-season superstar with outstanding flavor and large heads that weigh in the range of 3 to 5 pounds. Because it needs a long season to mature, it's planted in early summer and allowed to grow through summer and autumn and into winter, with the sweet flavor intensifying as the mercury plunges. The colors also deepen as winter nears; the large green leaves develop eye-catching purple-pink markings. Gardens in Zone 6 and warmer can get away with a light winter mulch to protect the heads; in colder regions, mulch with straw or shredded leaves and top with a mini hoop tunnel. Harvest as needed.

'COEUR DE BOEUF' (65–70 days), This is a good choice for setting out in spring, as the funny pointed heads are ready just 2 months from planting. The heads aren't as dense as rounded varieties, but the flavor and unique shape set them apart. Also, I appreciate a cabbage that yields the perfect amount for a family meal with no waste!

'KALIBOS' (85–100 days). Not quick to mature, but among the most beautiful cabbages you'll ever see! 'Kalibos' is an heirloom variety that yields good-size, reddish purple, cone-shaped heads. The plants are extremely ornamental, with large greenish purple outer leaves and fully purple heads. I've always been a sucker for a cone-shaped cabbage, and this one is easy to grow, with heads that are dense and sweet. We plant it in midsummer for a fall harvest.

'Coeur de Boeuf'   'Kalibos'

'January King'

like broccoli?

try these!

'Piracicaba'

'Spigariello Liscia'

Romanesco

Unfortunately for my kids, we eat broccoli at least three times a week — sometimes more! They tolerate it, but they don't have a deep affection for it like I do.

If you're a broccoli fan like me, though, you're definitely going to want to add a few of the following broccoli-like vegetables to your garden. 'Spigariello Liscia' broccoli is one. It's not your conventional supermarket broccoli — heck, I don't think you'd even find it at large-scale farmers' markets — and it's grown for its broccoli-flavored leaves. Yes, *leaves*, not flower buds.

Or how about sea kale? It yields large broccoli-like buds as well as kale-like foliage, but you're not going to see it next to cauliflower and cabbage at the grocery store. Another favorite is Romanesco broccoli, which has incredibly complex heads with tiny, mesmerizing swirls. They're also delicious, with a mild, nutty flavor that takes very well to roasting. Happily, most of these are very easy to grow, demanding just sunshine, fertile soil, and regular moisture.

'Spigariello Liscia' Broccoli

BROCCOLI LOVERS WILL APPRECIATE this Italian leaf-type relative that is grown primarily for its broccoli-flavored leaves. 'Spigariello Liscia' is a true broccoli, unlike broccoli raab, which is a member of the turnip family (hence, its strong flavor). The broccoli flavor of 'Spigariello Liscia' has overtones of kale, as well as a texture that is similar to some of the more tender kale varieties, like 'Lacinato'. The plants will eventually produce small edible florets, but it's those beautiful blue-green leaves that make this a green worth growing.

GROWING

'Spigariello Liscia' should be grown like broccoli; give it a 4- to 6-week head start by sowing the seeds under grow lights indoors. In the garden, space them about 18 inches apart, planting in compost-enriched soil in a sunny garden bed. Alternatively, direct sow seed 2 weeks before the last expected spring frost, spacing 2 inches apart. Thin to 18 inches when seedlings are growing well. For a fall crop, start seedlings indoors in early summer and transplant them into the garden about 10 weeks before your first expected fall frost.

If cabbageworms are a common problem in your garden, cover seedlings with a lightweight row cover right after planting. The cover can be left on the entire growing season; the plants don't need to be pollinated to produce their crop of leaves and baby buds.

EATING!

Pick individual leaves as needed. The young flower buds (or even edible yellow flowers) can also be harvested as a secondary crop. Prep the leaves for cooking by de-stringing them; the tough center ribs can be sliced out with a knife, but it's quicker (and more fun) to gently fold the leaves and pull the rib out — just like the string on a bean or pea. Use the chopped leaves as you would kale in Italian soups (it's great in bean soups), or like spinach in lasagna. It's also great wilted in a quick sauté with olive oil and garlic or slivered into robust fall salads.

THE DETAILS

A.K.A.: Leaf broccoli, *Brassica oleracea* var. *italica*

DAYS TO MATURITY: 45 days for leaves, 70 days for flower buds

HAILS FROM: Mediterranean region

VARIETY TO TRY: 'Spigariello Liscia'

'Spigariello Liscia'

'Piracicaba' broccoli

'Piracicaba' Broccoli

AT THE RISK OF SOUNDING a little like a used car salesman, "Have I got a broccoli for you!" It's the perfect broccoli for people who don't like broccoli. And those who already love this nutrient-dense veggie will have a new favorite for their gardens. 'Piracicaba' broccoli was developed in Brazil and is heat tolerant, frost tolerant, easy to grow, and incredibly productive. and it has a mild, sweet flavor that has to be tried to be believed.

Unlike regular broccoli that forms a large, tight dome of teeny beads, this is grown for its long harvest of tender side shoots, as well as the edible leaves. The side shoots differ slightly in appearance from those on typical garden broccoli; they're looser in form with noticeably large beads. The plants are also a little more casual in appearance, growing 2 to 3 feet tall and wide, with a more relaxed growth habit.

PLANT FOR SUMMER AND WINTER HARVEST

Grow 'Piracicaba' the same way you would grow regular broccoli, as detailed in the description for 'Spigariello Liscia' (see page 153). Plant in full sun, in compost-amended beds, and protect from common broccoli pests like cabbageworms.

'Piracicaba' holds well into the summer and will continue to pump out months of high-quality, bite-size flower buds. Regular harvesting will encourage continual cropping, as will regular moisture and an occasional dose of fish emulsion.

Sow a fall crop indoors in early summer and move the plants into the garden 10 to 12 weeks before the first expected fall frost. With the protection of a mini hoop tunnel, my 'Piracicaba' remains harvestable into December.

TENDER SHOOTS AND LEAVES

The first harvest comes from the center head, a modest 2-inch-wide flower bud that should be removed to initiate side-shoot production. As the side shoots develop, you can remove them individually or by cutting a 6- to 8-inch-long cluster of shoots and leaves. These can be steamed, stir-fried, or cooked in the same way as broccoli or broccoli raab. Unlike broccoli raab, however, the flavor of 'Piracicaba' remains sweet and mild.

Note that the tender florets need less cooking time than those of regular broccoli and need to be steamed for only a minute or two. Don't forget that the leaves are edible — and delicious! 'Piracicaba' produces more leaves than common garden broccoli, so expect a generous harvest. The stems can also be eaten, or grated into slaw. They, too, have a mild, sweet flavor.

THE DETAILS

A.K.A.: *Brassica oleracea* var. *italica*

DAYS TO MATURITY: 80 days from direct seed, 56 days from transplant

HAILS FROM: Mediterranean region

VARIETY TO TRY: 'Piracicaba'

Romanesco Broccoli

THE DETAILS

A.K.A.: Roman cauliflower, broccoflower, *Brassica oleracea* var. *botrytis*

DAYS TO MATURITY: 80 days

HAILS FROM: Mediterranean region

VARIETIES TO TRY: 'Veronica', a hybrid more reliable and disease resistant than the standard Romanesco; 'Gitano'

WITH ITS MESMERIZING, COMPLEX, spiraling heads, this is arguably the most visually appealing member of the broccoli clan. It also has a knockout flavor that is mild and almost nutty — reminiscent of both its relatives, broccoli and cauliflower. In truth, Romanesco broccoli is neither broccoli nor cauliflower, but is in a class all its own! Since cauliflower is one of my favorite vegetables, I tend to cook this crop in a similar way; roasted into caramelized, crispy bites, it rivals potato chips as an addictive snack.

Since I'm being totally honest, though, I will say that — like cauliflower — Romanesco broccoli isn't the easiest crop to grow. It's prone to buttoning (producing tiny heads), cabbageworms, slugs, and just general sulking. For pure novelty and flavor, though, it's worth a try!

ELBOW ROOM AND GENTLE HANDLING

Start these as you would broccoli, seeding them indoors 6 to 8 weeks before the last expected frost, eventually moving them to a sunny garden bed amended with plenty of compost. I avoid manure, as excess nitrogen can prevent Romanesco from heading up. With regular broccoli, I sow the seeds in cell packs, but in the case of Romanesco, I prefer 4-inch pots, which give them plenty of room to grow and develop into good-size plants, about 6 inches tall. When you're ready to transplant, minimize setback by not disturbing the rootball and watering them in immediately.

The plants get big, so spacing is important. Planting them too close can result in small or no heads, so plant them at least 1½ to 2 feet apart. Use the empty space between the tiny seedlings to interplant a quick-growing crop of leaf lettuce, radishes, or Japanese turnips.

I prefer to grow Romanesco as a fall crop, because I find the plants are more successful as the temperature begins to decline and there are (knock on wood) fewer pests. For a fall crop, start seeds indoors, 10 to 12 weeks before your last expected frost, and move them to the garden in midsummer. Water often and mulch with shredded leaves or straw.

Harvest entire heads while they are slightly immature (about 6 inches in diameter) and are still firm to the touch. Eat them raw (dipped in anything!) or roasted in the oven until they are lightly browned.

Romanesco

TRY THIS!
Gai Lan

I CAME TO GROW GAI LAN in our gardens because I found it hard to source locally. And trust me, this isn't a vegetable you want to be without. It's extremely versatile in the kitchen and super quick to prepare. One of my favorite ingredients in stir-fries and fried rice, it can also stand on its own as a flavorful side dish. The plants look like broccoli on a diet; they're about half the height, up to 16 inches tall, and are more slender than typical broccoli plants. This makes gai lan an especially great choice for small-space gardeners.

If the name "gai lan" doesn't sound familiar, perhaps you know this popular vegetable as Chinese broccoli, white-flowering broccoli, kailaan, or Chinese kale. Gai lan is harvested as a shoot with thick stems, large blue-green leaves, and small flower buds. It tastes like broccoli, but slightly stronger, and is generally not bitter. I say "generally," because if plants are left in the garden too long, the flavor can sharpen and acquire a mild peppery zing.

WAIT FOR BUDS, THEN HARVEST

Gai lan is grown the same way as broccoli, but it's easier and more reliable, and it adapts to a wider range of growing conditions. Start the seeds indoors and move them to the garden 4 to 5 weeks later. Give them full sun and rich soil, with a 10- to 12-inch spacing. In areas prone to drought, water regularly for the best-quality crop and apply an organic mulch to discourage weeds and retain soil moisture.

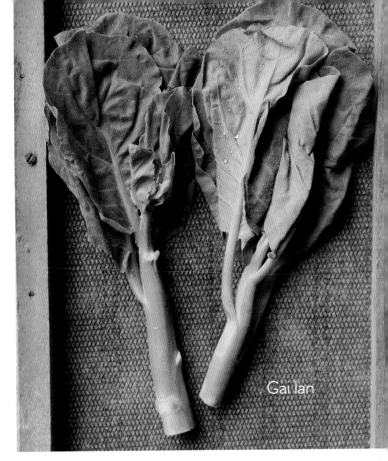

Gai lan

You can pick the plants bud-free as baby gai lan, but we prefer to wait until the main stem is topped with small clusters of flower buds. When the buds appear, snip about 8 inches of the stem with several leaves still attached. Then leave the plant to regrow (a little fish emulsion fertilizer is a good idea at this time); it will continue to push out smaller side shoots for a few weeks.

The easiest — and perhaps the best — way to serve this versatile crop is "Hong Kong style." This starts with a quick stir-fry in a tablespoon or two of garlic- and ginger-infused oil. After 2 to 3 minutes, add a splash of vegetable or chicken broth and cover the pan to allow the fragrant mixture to steam for 4 to 5 minutes. Drain and drizzle with oyster sauce and sesame oil. Seriously good.

THE DETAILS

A.K.A.: Chinese broccoli, Chinese kale, kai-lan, kailaan, *Brassica oleracea* var. *alboglabra*

DAYS TO MATURITY: 60–70 days

HAILS FROM: Mediterranean region

VARIETIES TO TRY: 'Green Jade' and 'Green Lance' give a more uniform harvest; 'Green Lance' is 10 days earlier than open-pollinated varieties.

TRY THIS!
Sea Kale

THE DETAILS

A.K.A.: *Crambe maritima*

DAYS TO MATURITY:
Perennial in
Zones 5–9

HAILS FROM:
European coast
(Atlantic)

VARIETY TO TRY:
Consider trying the
related giant colewort.

WHEN IS KALE NOT KALE? When it's sea kale, of course! Sea kale is an ancient member of the cabbage family that has been embraced by modern permaculturalists who appreciate its hardiness, longevity, and numerous edible parts, including florets that can be harvested and eaten like broccoli. It has a relaxed growing habit, forming a 2- to 3-foot-tall spreading mound with large silvery green leaves that are tinged with purple.

Although it's called sea kale, and is indeed salt tolerant, it grows very well in a regular vegetable bed. You can tuck some into a mixed border or flower garden, where it will return year after year and produce tiny, white, fragrant flowers that are highly attractive to pollinators and beneficial insects.

SLOW BUT RELIABLE

This is not a quick-growing plant, but once it's established, it will be a reliable, drought-tolerant, low-maintenance perennial. It's hard to find transplants for sea kale at garden centers and nurseries, but you can easily source seeds through online catalogs. Sow them indoors at least 8 to 10 weeks before the last expected frost. However, germination rates are typically very low, in the 20 to 30 percent range, so plant more seeds than you think you will need. Germination can also be very slow, taking several weeks.

As the seedlings grow, transplant them into 6-inch pots. In late fall of the first year, move them into a greenhouse, cold frame, or mini hoop tunnel to overwinter. Or plant them in the garden and mulch them with a deep layer of straw or shredded leaves.

Remember that this is a perennial plant, so find a spot that meets its needs: full sun to partial shade, and excellent soil drainage. Raised beds work very well for sea kale. Keep established plants happy with a fall application of rotted manure or compost.

WAIT, THEN HARVEST

As with asparagus, another popular perennial crop, resist harvesting the spring shoots of sea kale for the first 2 years. You can pick the summer leaves (eat like kale or 'Spigariello Liscia' broccoli) and immature flower buds (eat like broccoli), but don't disturb the spring growth. By year 3, you can start harvesting those tender shoots when the plants emerge in early spring. Traditionally, shoots are covered with a cachepot or a bucket to blanch them (and force them to produce an earlier crop). After forcing, allow the plant to grow naturally. You can continue to eat the young leaves, but as the season progresses and the plants switch to flowering, the foliage quickly toughens up. Harvest the flower buds in summer before they open and prepare them like broccoli.

TRY THIS!
Huauzontle

ALSO CALLED AZTEC SPINACH, this ancient quinoa cousin originates from Mexico and offers a variety of edible parts: leafy greens, quinoalike grains, and dense clusters of flower buds that you can cook and eat like broccoli. The flavor of huauzontle (pronounced wah-zont-lay) does hint of broccoli, but it also has a peppery kick and undertones of spinach.

To grow huauzontle, start the seeds indoors 4 to 5 weeks before the last expected frost, or direct seed in mid-spring, when the soil has warmed to 50°F (10°C). The seeds are small, so just scatter them on the soil surface and gently tamp them down to ensure good soil-seed contact. Aim to space them about 3 inches apart. Once they've emerged and are growing well, thin the plants to 12 inches apart. Water weekly if there has been no rain, and fertilize occasionally with a fish emulsion.

Like quinoa and amaranth, the young leaves can be picked and eaten throughout the growing season. Harvest individual leaves as needed, taking no more than one-quarter at a time. Overharvesting can delay the production of flower buds. Use the leaves like you would spinach: raw in salads and sandwiches; cooked in curry, stir-fries, dips, and gratins. The plants will grow quite tall, 4 to 5 feet, and by midsummer the large clusters of flower buds will emerge. The bud clusters can be steamed or boiled as you would broccoli.

You can turn the bud clusters into fritters, a traditional Mexican dish eaten during Lent. To make them, begin by removing the florets from the stems. This can be a time-consuming process, but one that is made quicker with several sets of hands. Once de-stemmed, rinse the florets with a fine-mesh strainer under running water and boil for 8 to 10 minutes. They should be bright green after cooking, but tender. These can be mixed with Mexican cheese and dipped into an egg-based batter and fried. The fritters are served on a bed of tomato sauce.

THE DETAILS

A.K.A.: *Chenopodium nuttalliae*

DAYS TO MATURITY: 80 days

HAILS FROM: Mexico

VARIETIES TO TRY: None

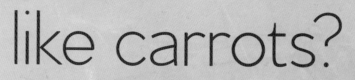

like carrots?

grow unusual varieties

'Lunar White'

'Yellowstone'

'Red Samurai'

'Atomic Red'

'Cosmic Purple'

'Atomic Red'

GROWING UP, I THOUGHT CARROTS were all orange. In fact, the original wild carrot from which all others are descended was actually white, forked, and spindly. Somewhere along the way, the roots of the wild carrot were transformed into those of the sweet orange carrot gardeners today know and love. That journey is thought to have taken around a thousand years, with the first domesticated carrots probably being purple or yellow. Orange carrots are the result of relatively modern breeding and likely resulted from crosses with yellow carrots about 400 years ago.

It's only in recent years that colored carrots have made a comeback, showing off their bold array of colors as well as subtle flavor differences. We plant several beds and cold frames of carrots each spring, as well as in midsummer for a fall and winter harvest. Like most gardeners, we grow a handful of orange varieties, but we also love to experiment with the many white, red, yellow, and purple carrots now found in seed catalogs. Gardeners with less space can buy premixed packets of rainbow carrots, but I like to blend my own by picking my favorite varieties and mixing them together.

Everyone loves to taste test our rainbow carrots, trying to detect how the flavors change from one color to the next. Purple carrots have a sweetness, but they often have a spicy hint of pepper, too. Red carrots taste similar to orange carrots but are slightly less sweet. White and yellow carrots are mild with fewer sugars than orange varieties, and little of the earthiness often associated with carrots.

TRY THIS!
Colorful, Craveworthy Carrots

'ATOMIC RED' (75 days). My kids call these "tomato carrots" — not because of their dazzling coral-red color, but because I've told them that the roots contain lycopene, an antioxidant that gives fruits like watermelon and tomatoes their characteristic red hue. 'Atomic Red' carrots have become a favorite in our garden and have proven to be reliable and easy to grow. The Imperator-type roots will grow 8 to 10 inches long and have a mildly sweet taste that deepens after frost.

'PUSA ASITA BLACK' (75 days). This dramatic purple-black carrot was developed in India, with nutrient-dense roots high in anthocyanins, which give them their dark color. The mildly sweet, earthy flavor is definitely best after a frost, so be patient and plant them for a fall and winter harvest. The roots grow 5 to 6 inches long. Be warned that the color bleeds into cooked dishes; so they're not good for the soup pot, unless you like purple soup! Enjoy the roots raw — they look amazing when grated with orange carrots for a slaw or salad — or steam, stir-fry, or roast them by themselves. It's open-pollinated and biennial, so let a few of the roots overwinter for seed collecting the following summer.

'COSMIC PURPLE' (70 days). One summer, when my daughter was about 6 years old, she decided that she only wanted to eat purple vegetables. Sigh. We muddled

'Pusa Asita Black'

'Yellowstone'

to 7 inches long and have a sweet, slightly spicy flavor. The dark purple skin contrasts nicely with the bright orange core, and the thin skin doesn't need to be peeled; just scrub and eat!

'PURPLE DRAGON' (70 days). Purple on the outside, orange on the inside, 'Purple Dragon' is a beautiful carrot with slender 6- to 7-inch-long roots. It was bred by noted American breeder Dr. John Navazio. Like many dark-colored carrots, this variety has a pleasing combination of sweet-spicy flavor; it's also rich in anthocyanins and contains lycopene. To take full advantage of the cool color combination, slice the roots into coins for dipping in hummus or for stir-fries.

'WHITE SATIN' (70 days). One of the most popular and widely available white carrots, 'White Satin' has smooth, slender roots that grow 7 to 9 inches long and are uniformly white throughout. Their flavor is mild but sweet; we like to roast these with a bit of honey or maple syrup for a tasty treat! These have been very popular with the kids, so I plant them in our winter cold frames, as well as in the spring and summer garden.

'JAUNE OBTUSE DU DOUBS' (70 days). This sunny yellow French heirloom will brighten up any carrot patch. The 6- to 8-inch-long roots are thick, sweet, and crisp with a strong carrot flavor. They taste great raw and are particularly appealing in salads or sliced with other veggies for dipping.

'LUNAR WHITE' (75 days). When I pulled the first few roots of 'Lunar White', my initial thought was that they looked like slender parsnips. They were 7 to 9 inches long with pale white skin and a matching white core. They have a mellow sweetness; we like them raw in salads, or roasted in the oven,

through and discovered that there are actually *a lot* of purple veggies: tomatoes, potatoes, kohlrabi, eggplant, peas, beans, peppers, cabbage, and her top pick, carrots. 'Cosmic Purple' has been growing in our garden ever since. The roots grow

which enhances the sweet flavor. When grown under drought conditions, that core can get woody, so be sure to water weekly if there has been no rain.

'PURPLE HAZE' (75 days). This All-America Selections winner is among the most popular of the colored carrots, yielding 8- to 10-inch-long deep purple roots with pumpkin orange interiors. They're sweet, with a welcome crunch. Interestingly, the deepest color will come from roots grown in cool conditions — in the range of 60 to 68°F (15 to 20°C); we have good luck with our spring crop, but it's our late-autumn harvest that gives us the darkest carrots. The roots will grow up to 12 inches long and have a 1½- to 2-inch shoulder. If boiled or added to soup or stew, the purple color will fade (and give cooked dishes a muddy purple hue), but 'Purple Haze' carrots are perfect for raw dishes or stir-fries.

'YELLOWSTONE' (72 days). This is a Danvers-type carrot with 1- to 2-inch shoulders and medium-long roots that taper to a sharp point. They'll get 7 to 8 inches long and have bright yellow skin with pale yellow flesh that is sweet with a mild earthiness. We love them grated with purple, red, and orange varieties, as well as a big handful of Italian parsley, for a dazzling salad.

'RED SAMURAI' (70 days). A Japanese variety, 'Red Samurai' yields long, slender roots with smooth, watermelon red skin and reddish pink flesh. They will usually grow 11 inches long, but in good soil, they can reach lengths of up to 14 inches. The unusual color is retained during cooking, but you can also eat them raw, enjoying their sweet-peppery flavor.

growing great carrots

> Carrots need a sunny site and deep, weed-free, stone-free soil with a fine, friable surface. If that doesn't sound like your garden, consider building a raised bed. Dig in 2 to 3 inches of compost. Avoid high-nitrogen fertilizers, as excessive nitrogen will cause roots to fork or become hairy.

> Sow seed 2 to 3 weeks before the last expected spring frost. Carrot seed is small, so take your time sowing to reduce the need to thin later on. Sow in shallow trenches, spacing the seeds every ½ inch and rows 8 to 10 inches apart. Cover lightly with soil (about ½ inch) and water the bed. Keep the soil evenly moist until the seeds germinate, which will take 1 to 2 weeks.

> Once the seedlings are growing well, thin them to 2 inches apart. As the carrots grow, continue to thin by pulling every second root. This allows the remaining ones to thicken up. Don't forget to eat the thinnings!

> Irrigate weekly with a deep soaking to encourage steady growth, and pull any weeds that appear.

> Succession plant by sowing fresh seed every 3 to 4 weeks. Our last planting is our winter crop, which we sow the first week of August — 10 to 12 weeks before the first expected fall frost.

> Keep an eye out for pests like the carrot rust fly and slugs, which are drawn to carrot seedlings like a magnet. I use diatomaceous earth to discourage the slugs. Deer also love carrot greens, so protect your crop with a fence or barrier.

> Mulch the soil with shredded leaves or straw to hold in soil moisture but also to prevent green shoulders.

> To avoid breaking off carrot tops and leaving the roots stuck in the ground at harvest time, use a garden fork to loosen the earth before you start tugging on the tops.

> Wait to harvest autumn carrots until cold weather has turned the starches in the roots to sugar. (Our kids call them "garden candy!")

> The tops of your homegrown carrots can be eaten raw or cooked. They have a bitter flavor, so we blanch them to temper the bitterness, and then stir-fry with a bit of garlic and olive oil.

like beets?

'Yellow Cylindrical'

grow unusual varieties

Earthy, sweet, hand-staining beets offer a dual harvest of tender roots and fresh greens, which can be steamed, sautéed, or used to replace chard or spinach in your favorite dishes. ('Bull's Blood' is a red-leafed variety that makes a beautiful and tasty baby salad green.) However, most gardeners grow beets for their round red roots, which have a sweet, earthy flavor.

Red beets are a garden standard, but that doesn't mean it's not fun to experiment with the various unusual types of beets. From the pale colors and mild flavors of golden and white varieties, to the incredibly sweet sugar beets, to the ancient 'Red Crapaudine', there are some wonderful beets for adventurous gardeners to try.

TRY THIS!
Rustic, Flavorful 'Red Crapaudine'

GIVEN ITS RUSTIC APPEARANCE, you probably won't be surprised to learn that 'Red Crapaudine' is an ancient vegetable, often called "the oldest beet in cultivation." To be perfectly honest, it was that claim that

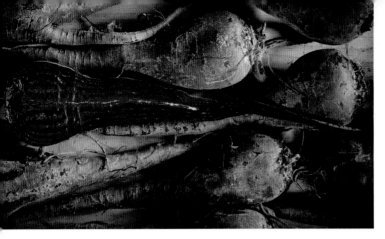

first tempted me to grow this rare variety. Well, that and the fact that Leslie Land, former garden columnist for the *New York Times*, called it "a heritage variety that even looks pre-modern from its fat carrot shape to its rough, bark-like skin. Of all the many beets I've grown, 'Red Crapaudine' is the tastiest, dense fleshed and sweet, with just enough — i.e., only a little — of beet's classic earthy taste."

As Land notes, this unusual variety does form long, conical roots, much like a carrot, but the thick, rugged skin is almost black in color, similar to a black Spanish radish (see page 192), and the roots are rarely uniform in size or shape. Sometimes they're forked, sometimes they're tiny, but most grow to a usable size in around 3 months. They also don't heave out of the soil, as some beets do, but typically remain buried.

The thick skin is a bit challenging to peel, but it does protect the sweet roots from all manner of weather, and they're a good choice for cold-season harvesting, suited to deep mulching, cold frames, or hoop houses. We don't bother peeling 'Red Crapaudine'; we find it easier to roast the roots whole and then slide the skin off the deep red flesh.

The foliage is extremely ornamental: deep green with blood-red stems and veins.

In habit, the foliage grows more out than up, and the young leaves are nice when served raw in salads, while the mature foliage can be sautéed, steamed, or stir-fried.

GROWING 'RED CRAPAUDINE'

These beets have a longer growing season than most other varieties, needing up to 3 months to mature. They can be planted in early spring for a summer crop or in midsummer for a fall and winter crop. I grow them for the cold season, finding better root quality when they're grown into autumn and harvested in cold weather. Yet no matter which season we have grown them, 'Red Crapaudine' roots are never woody or stringy.

Spotty germination rates are a common complaint, but this is likely due to inconsistent watering, as well as the fact that unlike most beet seeds, which are dried fruits with 2 to 4 seeds each, the fruits of 'Red Crapaudine' are single seeds. Direct sow in early spring, picking a sunny site with decent, well-drained soil. Raised beds are ideal. Work in a few inches of compost or aged manure and make shallow rows about 1 foot apart. Plant the seeds 1 inch apart, eventually thinning to a distance of 6 inches.

LOOSEN, THEN PULL

When it's time to harvest 'Red Crapaudine', use a pitchfork to loosen the soil around the plants before you try to pull them. The long roots hold tightly to the earth and don't come out easily when tugged. This French heirloom is a long keeper that stores for months in a root cellar or cold storage.

'Red Crapaudine' roots are neither uniform nor comely, but their rich flavor and firm texture set them apart and have made them a coveted crop for foodies.

Sugar
beet

Sugar Beets

ME TO THE KIDS: "We should plant sugar beets."

Kids to me: "YES!"

I guess it's not a surprise that kids would get excited about a vegetable with the word "sugar" in its name, and sugar beets are sweet — 16 to 20 percent of its weight comes from sucrose — but it still has the rugged, earthy flavor of the typical common beet. My main reason for growing sugar beets was so I could say "been there, done that" rather than hoping for a gourmet vegetable (which they're not) or the idea of producing our own sugar. Who has time for that?

Sugar beets are certainly an interesting crop to try, though, and the roots can reach mammoth proportions, weighing 2 to 4 pounds each! They have an ice-cream cone shape with white skin and flesh. They do take a long time to reach maturity, needing up to 90 days from seeding. If you have a little extra space, why not give them a try?

GROWING GREAT BIG SUGAR BEETS

Sow seeds 2 to 3 weeks before the last expected spring frost in a sunny site with fertile, well-drained soil. Before planting, loosen the soil to at least a foot to remove any clods of soil, rocks, or roots that could impede root growth; remember, sugar beets are big! Also, dig in a few inches of compost or aged manure.

Direct seed, spacing seeds 1 inch apart, thinning to a foot once the plants are a few inches tall. Giving them plenty of space will encourage large beets. Sugar beets need regular, even soil moisture to grow high-quality roots. Give plants 1 to 2 inches of water per week, and mulch with shredded leaves or straw to conserve moisture. Pull weeds as they appear.

Sugar beets are tolerant of cold weather and can be deep mulched with straw to extend the harvest into late autumn.

MAKE YOUR OWN SUGAR SYRUP

Harvest by loosening the earth with a garden fork, then gently pulling the big roots out of the soil. We get a lot of oohs and aahs when each beet is lifted from the garden bed. But what to do with sugar beets?

We weren't overly fond of the raw flavor of these beets, which can be grated and added to salads — it's a funny sweet-earthy flavor — but they were pretty good roasted in the oven with other root vegetables. The eating quality doesn't measure up to garden varieties, but we wanted to try and get as much out of these big beets as possible.

Making sugar is a time-consuming, fussy process, but making a sugar syrup is quite easy. Grate or thinly slice the roots, boiling them in a pot of water until the liquid thickens up. Strain and store in jars in the fridge. Use the liquid beet syrup as a sugar replacement in recipes, or add a dollop to iced tea, lemonade, tea, coffee, or cocktails.

The foliage of sugar beets is also edible, but it's thicker and a bit stringier than the typical garden beet. However, their young leaves cook up fine and can be sautéed, steamed, or stir-fried.

'Mammoth Red Mangel'

Sugar beets can grow quite large, but if you want to win a prize for biggest beet, I'd suggest you try growing 'Mammoth Red Mangel' (80 days). These monsters grow up to 2 feet long and can weigh in excess of 20 pounds! Obviously, they're not prime eating, but they can be fed to chickens and other livestock. Really fun for the kids!

'Blankoma'

'Albino'

TRY THIS!
White and Golden Beets

WHITE AND GOLDEN BEETS have become very popular with gardeners as they discover their mellow sweetness and muted, nutty flavor. Plus, they don't stain your hands (and clothes and counters and dish towels) when you clean and cook them. Pick them young as baby beets, or allow them to reach maturity for roasting, pickling, or boiling. If the roots of pale varieties heave out of the soil as they grow, their shoulders have a tendency green up. To remedy this, just shovel a bit of soil around the beets or mulch them with straw.

'ALBINO' (55 days). The round-rooted heirloom is quick to grow, ready just 8 weeks from seeding. The skin and flesh are a creamy white and have a sublime sweet flavor, popular even with folks who are not beet lovers. The bright green tops make excellent cooked greens.

'BLANKOMA' (55 days). This was the first white beet variety I tried in our gardens, and I was impressed. The seeds germinated quickly, and the plants grew well in both spring and fall. The roots are round, slightly conical, and pure white inside and out. The tops are vigorous and delicious!

'TOUCHSTONE GOLD' (55 days). One of my favorite golden varieties, this beet has reddish gold skin and a sunny yellow interior. Expect uniform roots, good germination, and vigorous green tops. Pick as a baby beet when the roots are just 1½ inches across, or let them grow to their mature size of 3 inches.

'BOLDOR' (51 days). Very quick to mature, 'Boldor' is a hybrid beet with reddish yellow skin and bright gold flesh. It's extremely consistent, producing uniform 2- to 3-inch diameter roots with an outstanding sweet flavor. Great for juicing.

'GOLDEN' (55 days). Here is a reliable heirloom with lemon yellow flesh and rosegold skin. Like other golden varieties, it has a sweet beet flavor, but the beets can get really big. We tend to pick these about 2 months from seeding when they are 2 to 4 inches across, but we've had a few that were 6 inches in diameter! With a little extra soil preparation, good weather, and a dose of luck, 'Golden' has the potential to produce giant-size roots.

'YELLOW CYLINDRICAL' (60 days). My mother is partial to cylindrical-shaped beets, which slice so nicely after roasting or boiling. We've grown the red variety 'Cylindra Formanova' for years, so when I noticed 'Yellow Cylindrical' listed in a seed catalog, I was anxious to give it a try. It's a mangel-type beet that is used primarily for animal feed, but that's when it's allowed to mature. We pick the oblong roots young and enjoy the bright gold skin and white flesh in our favorite beet recipes.

'Yellow Cylindrical'

like potatoes?

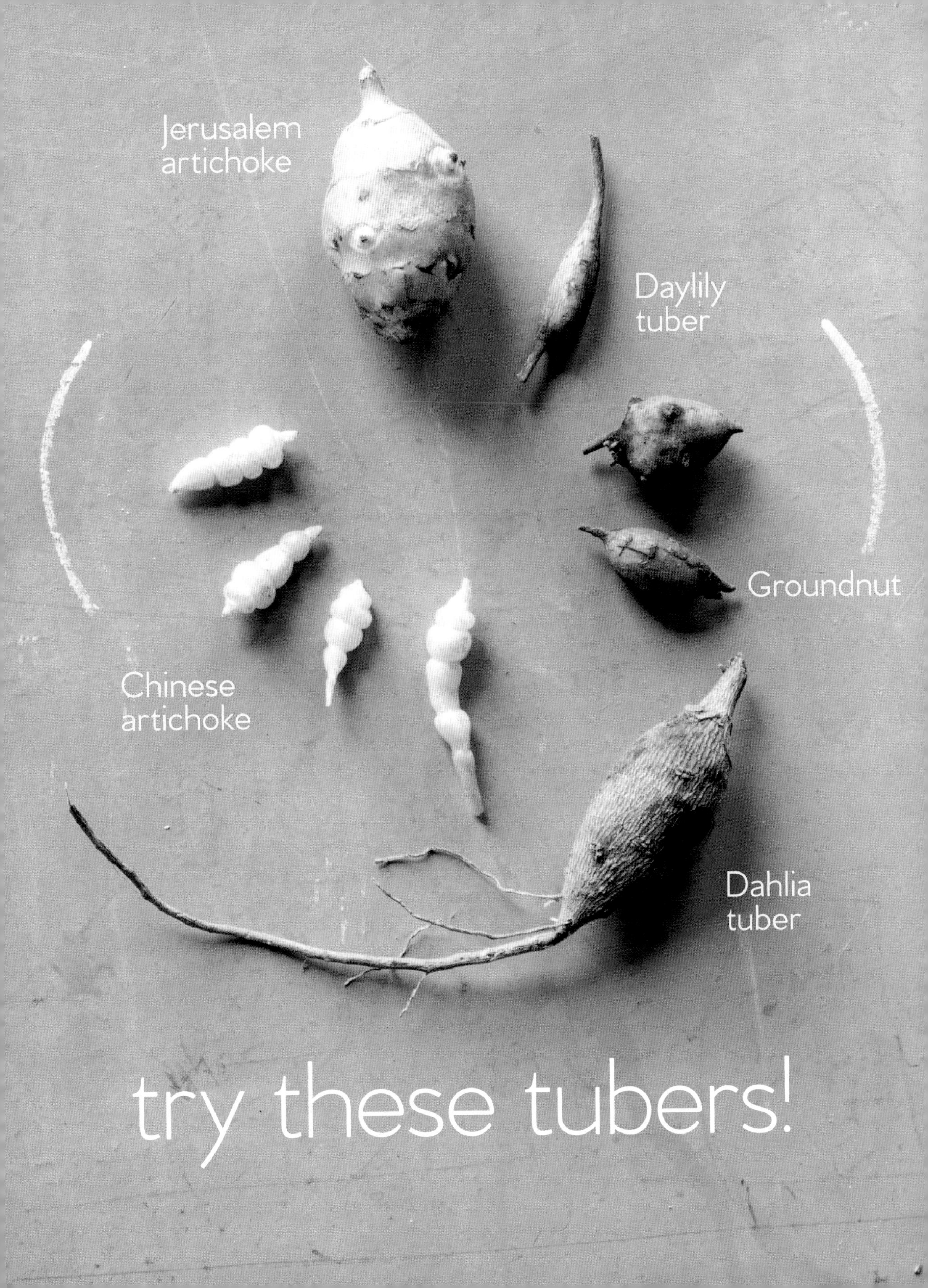

Jerusalem artichoke

Daylily tuber

Groundnut

Chinese artichoke

Dahlia tuber

try these tubers!

Confession time: For years (between the ages of 2 and 8), potatoes were probably the only vegetable I ate. Eventually my mother convinced me to try snap beans, and my love of veggies was sparked. However, potatoes have remained a firm favorite, and I dedicate as much garden space as I can to potatoes and potato-like crops.

There is something special about crops that grow beneath the soil; the harvest always feels like a treasure hunt, and even picking a few handfuls of potatoes for dinner becomes a family activity. With lesser-known crops like Chinese artichokes, it becomes even more of an event, as everyone wants to get a peek at the funny-looking tubers that resemble fat, white grubs.

Not all potato-like crops are annuals. Some, like groundnut and sunchoke, are perennials and offer years of reliable cropping. They've become popular among foragers and permaculturists, who appreciate their resilience and ease of cultivation. Now, I'm not saying you should forgo potatoes completely, but at least consider trying a few other crops that produce tasty, edible tubers.

Jerusalem Artichoke

JERUSALEM ARTICHOKE IS A perennial sunflower that is native to North America. It's grown for its potato-like tubers, but many gardeners also plant it for the small sunflower-like blooms that emerge in late summer. The tall plants can reach 9 feet and are easy to grow, resistant to most pests and diseases, and produce tasty tubers that can be harvested through autumn and winter. But (you knew there was a "but" coming, didn't you?), they can quickly cross the line from enthusiastic to invasive if left unchecked.

The best way to make sure they don't get out of hand is to pick the right site. You want a sunny spot with decent soil, and preferably one that is out of the way; perhaps along a fence or at the back of the garden. You can also grow them in raised, enclosed beds — or large containers, as I do — to control their spread. The downsides to growing sunchokes in pots are that the limited soil space of a container reduces the quantity of roots the plant produces, and you will need to bury the pots if you want to harvest into winter.

While you're weighing the pros and cons of Jerusalem artichokes, let me tell you about their tubers. They look a bit like gingerroot: knobby, 2 to 3½ inches long, and often light brown in color, although the color can range from white to red, depending on the variety. They have the fluffy texture of a potato but a mild artichoke or water chestnut flavor. The tubers contain inulin, a carbohydrate that is not broken down by our stomachs, and therefore can create excess amounts of, ahem, gas, giving this crop another nickname: "fartichoke." However, cooking, and particularly slow roasting, does convert some of the inulin into fructose. And harvesting and storing the roots for several weeks *before* eating also reduces the inulin quantity.

HERE COMES THE SUN(CHOKE)

Sunchokes are a long-season crop and are typically planted in the spring, a week or two before the last expected frost. Tubers are sold in garden centers, but if you have trouble sourcing them, ask at your local farmers' market or order them online.

Because these are aggressive plants, you should put some thought into picking a site. Look for an area where they won't be

THE DETAILS

A.K.A.: *Helianthus tuberosus*, sunchokes

DAYS TO MATURITY: Perennial in Zones 4–9

HAILS FROM: North America

VARIETIES TO TRY: 'Clearwater', 'Stampede', 'Skorospelka','Red Fuseau','Garnet'

'Red Fuseau'

'Garnet'

able to spread into nearby garden beds or neighboring properties. Sunchokes aren't too fussy about soil, but they do need full sun, especially if you want big tubers and late-summer flowers. Loosen the soil and amend with compost or aged manure to boost production. Avoid planting in wet soil, which would not only result in poor yields but could potentially kill the plants.

Plant the tubers 18 to 24 inches apart and 4 to 6 inches deep; this will encourage large rhizomes. You can plant them as little as a foot apart, although tuber size will decrease. Sunchokes are low-maintenance plants, but they do appreciate even moisture. If you're not too fussy about a large crop, just ignore the plants, and they'll survive. If you want a decent harvest, give them an inch or two of water each week and hill up the plants with compost or soil when they are 18 to 24 inches tall. Some gardeners also cut off the flowers to direct energy back to the tubers. The flowers are beautiful, though, and they attract and support late-summer and autumn pollinators, so we leave them. Trim faded flowers to prevent self-seeding.

DIGGING CHOKES

It's time to cut back the plants when the foliage has yellowed — usually after a few good hard frosts. If you don't plan on harvesting right away, leave the foliage on top of the bed as a mulch. The tubers can be dug all autumn and winter, but you'll need to top the bed with an additional 1 to 1½ feet of shredded leaves or straw to keep the ground from freezing. If you're ready to harvest, carefully lift the tubers with a garden fork.

There's usually no reason to replant; the missed tubers (and there will be some) will shoot up the following spring. However, if you want to be precise in your planting, try to dig up all the tubers, replanting medium-size ones at the recommended spacing.

Once dug, sunchokes will quickly soften and shrivel if they're not stored properly. Keep them in the fridge or a root cellar, where they can stay cool and moist to maintain quality for a few weeks. I find it best to leave them in the ground until we're ready to eat them.

When it comes to eating sunchokes, a little can go a long way. If you're new to this crop, start with a modest portion, making it a part, not the centerpiece, of your meal. Remember, it can and probably will cause gas.

Before eating, give the bumpy tubers a good scrub. Depending on the dish, they can be peeled before cooking or, if roasting or boiling, afterward. Once cooked, the skin is easier to remove and you'll have less waste. We treat them like potatoes, sautéing, steaming, baking, boiling, or frying them. You can also grate them and eat them raw in salads and other dishes.

TUBERS TO TRY

One of the common complaints about sunchokes is that once you peel the knobby roots, there is little left to eat. Newer varieties have been bred to have smoother roots that are easier to peel. There are hundreds of varieties, but here are some of the more commonly sourced sunchokes.

'CLEARWATER'. This is an early-maturing variety with light brown skin and white flesh. It has fewer "nubs" than most varieties, making peeling quick and easy.

'STAMPEDE'. This variety has smooth, almost knob-free tubers with golden skin and crisp, white flesh. This is an early-maturing variety that is ready to dig at least a month before other sunchokes.

'SKOROSPELKA'. Also early to mature, 'Skorospelka' is a Russian sunchoke with pinkish tan skin and white interiors. It produces fewer tubers than other varieties, but most are quite large.

'RED FUSEAU'. It's hard to resist these rose-red tubers! They're smooth and easy to peel, and they grow up to 4 inches long.

'GARNET'. Another red-skinned variety, 'Garnet' produces tubers that are more rounded in shape and mostly knob-free.

Get Some Groundnut

LIKE JERUSALEM ARTICHOKES, groundnuts are a perennial plant native to North America and often favored by foragers. Although it's in the bean family, its main crop comes from its peculiar rhizomes, which look like beads on a string. Each rhizome is about the size and shape of a walnut or a chicken egg, and to me, the flavor is kind of like a nutty potato, but with hints of turnip. The texture is also similar to that of potatoes, and they are usually boiled, steamed, roasted, baked, or fried like potatoes.

Grow it for the tubers, or grow it for the bright green foliage and large clusters of highly fragrant, maroon-ivory flowers. The pealike blooms appear in mid to late summer and are also edible. These are followed by green bean–like pods, which contain edible seeds. Unfortunately, my growing season isn't long enough to mature the seeds, but that's okay, as the tubers are the star of the show.

GROWING GROUNDNUT

In its natural habitat, groundnut is happiest when growing near streams, rivers, or marshes. It loves rich, moist soil and therefore will do just fine when planted in a damp spot. However, if you don't have a site with moist soil, it will still grow fine in regular loam, just be sure to dig in plenty of compost or aged manure before planting. You'll also need to provide a strong support like a fence, trellis, or arbor for the plants to climb. They can grow more than 10 feet in a single season, so be prepared for vigorous

THE DETAILS

A.K.A.: American groundnut, hopniss, potato bean, Indian potato, *Apios americana*

DAYS TO MATURITY: Perennial in Zones 4–9

HAILS FROM: North America

VARIETY TO TRY: 'Nutty'

vines. It's a good choice for an edible forest garden, spreading as a groundcover or climbing nearby trees and shrubs.

Tubers can be ordered in some seed catalogs; you might also find a container-grown plant at a native plant nursery. Or if you have a gardening friend with an existing vine, just ask for a few tubers. Plant them 2 to 3 inches deep in spring, as early as a few weeks before the last expected frost.

DIGGING ROOTS

Groundnut should be harvested in the autumn of its second year. You can dig a few small tubers the first year, but they'll only be about an inch in diameter. If you can wait until the following season, they will be egg-size. It's also a good idea to wait to harvest until the plants have been hit with frost and have died back. This will enhance the flavor of the tubers.

The swollen tubers lie just below the soil surface. Dig carefully until you find a string and then pull gently, loosening the soil with your hand or a tool, to expose the tubers. Don't overharvest! Make sure to leave a few tubers so that your plants will come back.

The protein-packed tubers (17 percent protein content) have a latexlike sap that makes the raw tubers bitter, so it's best to cook them. We like to boil them first and then pan-fry slices in a bit of olive oil. You can also add the boiled chunks to soups, stews, and other dishes. As with all new-to-you foods, start with a little to eliminate the possibility of an allergic reaction.

The young seedpods, which look like green beans, can also be eaten young. Once mature, the seeds inside can be shelled and dried for winter soups and other bean dishes. They need to be cooked thoroughly before being consumed.

TRY THIS!
Chinese Artichoke

WHEN I PROUDLY SHOWED THE KIDS my handful of just-picked Chinese artichokes, they said, "Ewww!" I can't blame them; they thought I was holding a pile of fat, white grubs. The ivory, spiraled tubers really do look like large larvae. Far from being grubs, though, they're a foodie favorite rarely seen at farmers' markets. Fortunately, they're quite easy to grow in a home garden.

A member of the mint family, Chinese artichoke forms edible tubers that grow 1 to 3 inches long. The odd-shaped tubers have a satisfying crunch and a mildly sweet flavor suggestive of water chestnuts; they can be eaten raw or cooked. The plants have bushy foliage and a wandering habit reminiscent of mint, and in midsummer they produce tall pinkish purple flower spikes that are attractive to pollinators and beneficial insects.

They're pretty enough for the flower border, but given their aggressive habit, I'd suggest planting them in pots or contained raised beds. In case you were wondering (given their lineage), this mint cousin sadly does not have aromatic or flavorful foliage.

CROPS OF CROSNES

Chinese artichokes (a.k.a. crosnes) aren't a common crop yet, but they are available through specialty seed catalogs and online. They are typically planted in early spring, a few weeks before the last expected frost. I got a jump on the growing season by starting mine indoors in 6-inch pots. Once the danger of frost had passed, I hardened them off and set them out in an isolated, compost-enriched garden bed, where they could roam to their hearts' content.

The plants need full sun to produce a good crop, especially in Zones 5 and 6. They also want rich, well-drained soil. Place the tubers 3 inches deep and 10 to 12 inches apart.

Small-space or no-space gardeners can grow crosnes in pots, but be sure to pick big pots — at least 15 inches across — and add some compost or aged manure to the potting mix. Stress from lack of moisture will reduce yield, so make sure to irrigate garden beds with an inch or two of water per week. Potted crosnes will likely need to be watered two or three times a week.

Crosnes respond well to shearing; once the plants are 1 foot tall, cut them down to 6 to 8 inches. As they grow back, shear them again. This will direct vegetative energy into tuber formation.

Although the plants are hardy to Zone 5, they don't yield tubers until late autumn. To help push things along, I erect a mini hoop tunnel over the bed in late September, keeping the ends open for air circulation. This means you'll need to water more diligently, but the extra shelter will help size up the tubers.

HARVEST IN AUTUMN

When the foliage dies back in autumn, the harvest can begin. As with Jerusalem artichokes, it's almost impossible to get all the tubers, but any that are left behind will pop up the following spring. Thin them to a foot apart at that time.

The most common complaint about Chinese artichokes is that they are difficult to clean. I use a vegetable brush to quickly scrub the dirt from the nooks and crannies.

The raw tubers can be eaten out of hand, but we prefer them cooked. The easiest way to cook them is to sauté the tubers in butter for a few minutes. You can also blanch the tubers in boiling water for 3 to 4 minutes, then slice them for salads. Just don't overcook them, as they'll quickly turn mushy. As with Jerusalem artichokes, if you're new to eating this crop, start with a little. A big helping of crosnes could to lead to gas.

In Japan, crosnes, called *chorogi*, are often pickled with purple perilla (see page 214), turning the white tubers bright red.

THE DETAILS

A.K.A.: Crosne (pronounced "crone"), *Stachys affinis*

DAYS TO MATURITY: Perennial in Zones 5–8

HAILS FROM: China

VARIETIES TO TRY: None

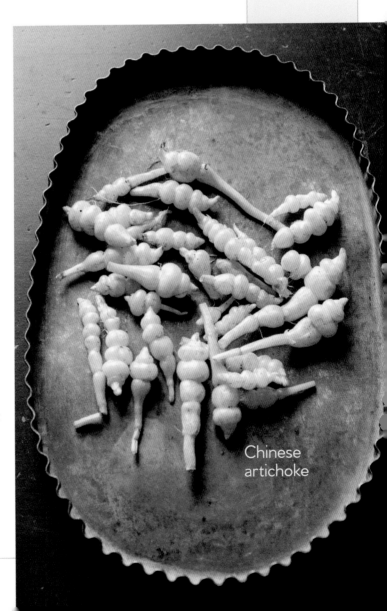
Chinese artichoke

Daylily Tubers

THE DETAILS

A.K.A.: Ditch lily,
Hemerocallis fulva

DAYS TO MATURITY:
Perennial in Zones
3–9

HAILS FROM: Asia

VARIETIES TO TRY:
There are a lot of
daylily cultivars out
there, but for culinary
purposes, stick to
H. fulva.

DAYLILIES ARE PERHAPS the perfect perennial. They're easy to grow, adapt to a wide variety of soil and light conditions, and are drought tolerant and insect resistant. Plus, they produce weeks of gorgeous flowers. And they're edible. We eat the flower buds, raw and cooked (see page 68), and add the opened blooms to salads, but another treasure is waiting beneath the soil surface: a bounty of tubers.

The tubers look like baby fingerling potatoes and are eaten raw or cooked. They have a crisp texture paired with a nutty sweetness that is nice when they are pan-fried or roasted until tender. There are tens of thousands of daylily cultivars, but for culinary purposes, I would recommend sticking to the regular orange ditch lily, *Hemerocallis fulva*. Please note that these are not true lilies (*Lilium* species), which are toxic.

SO EASY TO GROW

In some regions of the United States, ditch lilies are considered an invasive species for their ability to spread rapidly. Most cultivated forms of daylily are clump forming and don't become invasive. *H. fulva*, on the other hand, spreads by rhizomes and can form large colonies if unchecked.

As you may have guessed from the above warning, ditch lilies are easy to grow and happy in a wide variety of soils and light conditions. To encourage the largest harvest of tubers (or flower buds), plant them in good garden soil in full sun — perhaps in a raised bed where their enthusiastic growth can be contained?

The highest-quality tubers are harvested in late fall or very early spring. In summer, the tubers turn spongy and are not palatable. The tubers don't need to be peeled, but they will need a good scrubbing to remove any dirt. Once clean and patted dry, toss them with olive oil, sprinkle with salt and pepper, and roast them in the oven until fork-tender.

Some people (an estimated 5 percent of the population) have issues digesting day-lilies, so begin with a small quantity until you know whether you can tolerate this forager favorite.

Dahlias also have edible petals; sprinkle them on salads and other dishes for a pop of color!

TRY THIS!
Dahlia Tubers

WHEN I FIRST STARTED PLANTING DAHLIAS, I did it for the flowers. From tiny pompon to huge dinner-plate types, I've loved them all. Each spring, I would tuck clumps of tubers into our flower and vegetable beds to provide a long show of color and countless stems for cut flowers. Plus, the blooms are irresistible to pollinators! Come autumn, those tubers would be dug up again for winter storage, with the large clumps piled up on the soil like just-harvested potatoes. And like potatoes, the tubers of dahlias are edible.

Dahlias are a member of the sunflower family and are also related to Jerusalem artichokes. If you can't tolerant Jerusalem artichokes, you probably don't want to eat your dahlias. But if you do, keep in mind that of the tens of thousands of cultivars grown in gardens, not all make good eating; modern dahlias are bred for their flowers, not their tubers. However, dahlias were an important crop to the Aztecs and even as a food source in Europe as recently as several hundred years ago. Once the flowers became popular, though, the edible tubers were largely forgotten.

CRUNCHY AND MILD

Not all dahlia tubers taste good; some are bitter, some are bland, others have a sweet flavor with a crunchy texture or a mild flavor often compared to that of water chestnuts or celery. Food historian William Woys Weaver recommends the heirloom variety *Dahlia pinnata* 'Yellow Gem'. In my garden, dahlia tubers are not perennial (they're hardy to Zone 8 or 7 with protection) and need to be planted in mid-spring, when the soil temperature has reached 60°F (15°C). Look for a sunny site with decent soil, and dig in a few inches of compost or aged manure. Plant the clump 6 to 8 inches deep.

Once the plants have been touched by frost in autumn, it's time to dig the tubers for eating and storing. Lift the tubers, gently removing any dirt. Save some of the tubers for replanting, and use the rest for eating. Large clumps can be divided in fall or spring; just make sure to leave at least one eye on each clump. The eye is the part that will grow the foliage and flowers once planted. To overwinter tubers, store them in dry peat moss at 40 to 50°F (4 to 10°C). Check them periodically for rot, removing any affected tubers.

Grate or dice them raw in salads and slaws, where the crisp apple texture and celery-like flavor will shine. They can also be grated for baked goods like breads or muffins. Or roast or boil the tubers, eating them like potatoes. Chunks of diced tubers can also be added to soups and stews.

THE DETAILS
A.K.A.: *Dahlia pinnata*

DAYS TO MATURITY: 120–50 days, hardy to Zone 8 and above

HAILS FROM: Central and South America

VARIETY TO TRY: 'Yellow Gem'

WHY GROW ORDINARY POTATOES?

'All Red'

'La Ratte'

'Purple Peruvian'

'All Blue'

'Caribe'
(mature)

'AmaRosa'

'ALL RED' (80–90 days). Also known as 'Cranberry Red', this eye-catching potato has bright red skin with pinkish red flesh. It was developed by Robert Lobitz, a member of the Seed Savers Exchange, and introduced in 1984. The plants are extremely productive, bearing a heavy crop of medium to large tubers. 'All Red' is also scab resistant and drought tolerant.

'ALL BLUE' (80–90 days). Here's a potato that is purple on the outside *and* on the inside. The vibrant color resists fading when cooked, so boil it up and use it in a rainbow potato salad, or cut it into shoestrings and roast for purple French fries. Expect a good crop of medium-size tubers.

'PINK FIR APPLE' (100–110 days). These knobby pink tubers with yellow, waxy flesh have quickly become a family favorite at our house, and we plant them every year now. A bit of patience is required for this long-maturing crop, but when harvest time rolls around, you'll find the vigorous plants yield a generous harvest of long, slender, and very bumpy potatoes. After growing these for a few seasons, I learned that the plants produce many of their tubers close to the soil surface, so hill up the earth or lay down mulch midseason to protect shallow tubers from the sun.

'CARIBE' (65 days). We introduced purple-skinned 'Caribe' to our garden during the purple-vegetable phase my daughter, Isabelle, had a few years ago. We loved it so much that even when she (finally) outgrew her inclination for purple veggies, we kept on growing 'Caribe'. The tubers are oblong with amethyst-purple skin and moist, snow white flesh. It also stores well, lasting for several months in a cool, dark spot. Our favorite way to enjoy 'Caribe' is to steam or boil tubers until tender, then smash with the skins on. Add copious amounts of butter, salt, and pepper, and dig in!

'PURPLE PERUVIAN' (100 days). Almost too pretty to eat, these South American fingerlings produce long, slender, bumpy tubers with purple-black skin and dark purple interiors. The skin is thick and best peeled or slipped from the flesh after steaming. 'Purple Peruvian' makes very good french fries or roasted potatoes and retains its dramatic color after cooking.

'ARRAN VICTORY' (100–110 days). This is a Scottish heirloom with beautiful purple skin, milky white flesh, and great flavor. Unfortunately, the spectacular skin color fades with cooking, so cook lightly or roast with the skin on. The tubers are medium to large, and the plants consistently offer a higher than average yield.

'LA RATTE' (110 days). Who wouldn't want to grow a potato called 'La Ratte'? This marvelous French heirloom has a smooth, buttery texture that shines when steamed, boiled, or roasted. The long, slender tubers have light beige skin and ivory-yellow flesh, and are often knobby. The plants don't produce heavily, but the exceptional flavor is worth the modest harvest.

'AMAROSA' (110 days). The photo on the package of seed potatoes promised a dark red fingerling potato with equally dark red flesh. Everyone was so excited about this that even my teenage son helped with the planting (a miracle!). When it came time to dig them up, the plants yielded a heavy crop of dark red potatoes, but when we cut one open to inspect the flesh, it was more mottled pink-red than the hoped-for burgundy. We didn't mind for long though, as 'AmaRosa' was so good when baked as homemade french fries or boiled for bright red potato salad.

'All Blue'

'Caribe'

like spring radishes?

try winter radishes!

Watermelon
radish

'Green Luobo'

Who doesn't love spring radishes? So many colors, shapes and sizes, plus they're super easy to grow and ready just weeks from seeding. They're among the first crop sown in our cold frames in late winter, and also one of the first in the unprotected vegetable garden in April. Even the kids like to eat them!

Yet for all their outstanding qualities, spring varieties aren't the only worthwhile radishes to grow. We also love the winter types, which include daikons, black Spanish varieties, and 'China Rose'. Plus, there are radishes that are grown not for their roots but for their foliage or tender seed pods.

Radishes are members of the mustard family, hence the spicy kick offered by many varieties. There are two main types of radishes:

SPRING RADISHES. These are the cheerful, brightly colored round to oblong varieties, with a mild, peppery crunch. Grow them in hot or dry weather, however, and you'll find they go from mild to pungent

very quickly. Because they grow so quickly, they're a perfect vegetable for succession planting. We sow a pinch of fresh seed every few weeks so that we have a steady crop of spring radishes. Popular varieties include 'Easter Egg', 'Sparkler', 'Cherry Belle', 'French Breakfast', and 'Amethyst'.

WINTER RADISHES. Winter radishes need a longer growing season than spring types and are typically planted in mid to late summer for a fall or winter harvest. They hold their quality longer and better than spring radishes, have a deeper flavor profile, and they also can be mulched or grown in cold frames for late-fall and winter harvesting.

TRY THIS!
Delightful Daikon

DAIKON IS A WORKHORSE in the garden. Not only does it yield long, mild-flavored roots for fresh eating, cooking, and pickling, but it also improves soil structure by breaking up compacted clay and drawing nutrients up from deep within the soil.

Not all daikons grow long and slender; some are squat and bulbous, others round-rooted. And depending on the variety, some can grow exceptionally large. 'Sakurajima' is an heirloom variety that is considered to be the largest radish in the world, with round roots that, in the proper conditions, can grow up to 100 pounds! Of course, that's not its average size, which falls more in the range of 12 to 15 pounds with a 12-inch diameter.

Daikons also produce extremely vigorous tops, which can grow up to 2 feet across. As with other radishes, those leafy greens are edible; the seedpods are, too, as I learned a few years ago when winter came early and I still had a half-dozen daikons in the garden. Unfortunately, I hadn't mulched them and thought that I had missed my chance. However, the following spring, bright green foliage emerged from the overwintered roots, and I left them to grow, with the thought of seed saving. I didn't anticipate that each of the bolted plants would grow 5 feet tall and 3 feet across! They had very pretty soft purple flowers, followed by the characteristic pointed seedpods of radishes. The flowers were popular with the bees and beneficial insects, and we harvested both the flowers and pods for our salads.

DAIKON LIKES DEEP SOIL

Daikon needs full sun and deep, loose soil to produce high-quality roots. Raised beds are ideal. Clay or stony soil can result in stunted or forked roots. It's also a good idea to dig in some compost or rotted manure. Avoid high-nitrogen fertilizers, however, which will produce healthy tops but small roots.

As with other winter radishes, daikons grow best when planted for a fall crop. Direct seed in midsummer, spacing the seed 2 inches apart, eventually thinning to 6 inches. Rows should be 2 to 3 feet apart. Provide regular irrigation if there has been no rain.

If growing in containers, pick deep pots and grow short-rooted varieties like watermelon radishes. I find radishes in containers do best when grown in partial shade, where the soil won't dry out as quickly. To further help keep the soil moist, mulch container-grown daikons with straw once the plants are about 6 inches tall.

HARVEST WHEN THE SHOULDERS PUSH UP

When I first grew daikons, I thought it was best to leave them in the ground for as long as possible so that they could size up. Big mistake. The roots split and were woody and bitter. I've since learned that you should keep an eye on the crop and begin harvesting when the shoulders poke out of the soil, or close to the date that corresponds with the "days to maturity" listed on the seed packet.

THE DETAILS

A.K.A.: Giant white radish, lobok, Chinese radish, *mooli* (my favorite name), *Raphanus sativus*

DAYS TO MATURITY: 60–70 days

HAILS FROM: Mediterranean region, but cultivated in Japan and China for more than 1,200 years

VARIETIES TO TRY: 'Chinese Green Luobo', 'Miyashige', Watermelon radish

Daikon (along with cabbage) is a key ingredient in kimchi, the national dish of Korea. You can also eat them raw or bake, boil, roast, or stir-fry them. They're good in soups or grated for a condiment. The vigorous greens can be sautéed, stir-fried, or steamed like spinach.

DAIKONS TO DIG

'CHINESE GREEN LUOBO' (60 days). The roots of this Asian heirloom are unique: cylindrical with greenish gold skin and dark to light green flesh. They can grow big, but for the highest-quality roots, pull them when they're about 8 inches long. They're best seeded in mid to late summer for a fall or early-winter crop. The flavor hints of wasabi, which makes them a wonderful accompaniment to sushi. Their high-quality greens can be eaten raw in salads or lightly sautéed.

'MIYASHIGE' (60 days). This has been one of my favorite varieties for years. It's a "stump-rooted" daikon that grows 12 to 18 inches long and has white roots with green shoulders. The roots are mild and good for salads and fresh eating, as well as for fermenting and pickling. Sow in the summer for a fall crop, as it tends to bolt if planted in spring.

WATERMELON RADISH (a.k.a 'Shinrimei' or 'Red Meat' or 'Beauty Heart'; 60 days). Among the most beautiful of all radishes, the watermelon radish is becoming very popular in North American gardens and at farmers' markets. The name doesn't come from the flavor but from the appearance of the root: rounded with a light green exterior and neon pink flesh. This variety grows big — up to 4 inches across. It has a mild, slightly peppery, slightly sweet flavor and can be used in raw, cooked, or pickled dishes. It loses its unusual coloration when cooked, so I like to slice it raw for salads or vegetable trays or give it a brief stir-fry. For the sweetest roots, plant for a fall crop.

Watermelon radish

'Chinese Green Luobo'

TRY THIS!
Black Spanish
Radish

A.K.A.: *Raphanus sativus* var. *niger*

DAYS TO MATU-
RITY: 60 days

HAILS FROM:
Mediterranean

VARIETIES TO TRY:
'Nero Tondo', 'Long
Black Spanish'

"THAT IS HOT!" yelped my husband and his brother, Tony, when they tried a sliver of a just-pulled black Spanish radish. Lesson learned: this is definitely a radish that bites back. Raw, it livens up salads or partners well with a cold beer. Roasted, the pungency mellows, and it has a mild radish, almost turnip flavor.

There are two types of black Spanish radishes: one with round roots that grow 2 to 4 inches across, and one with elongated, carrotlike roots that grow 8 to 9 inches long. Both types have rough, inky black skin and icicle white flesh. The roots are very firm, When I first glanced at the coarse skin, my initial thought was that this is going to be a woody, inedible radish. However, when sliced open, the flesh was crisp and aromatic.

SOW FOR FALL

Black Spanish radishes can be planted in spring for a summer harvest, but being a winter-type radish, they grow best and have better flavor when they're planted in midsummer for fall and winter harvest. Spring-grown crops can be prone to bolting, especially if summer heat arrives early.

For a fall crop, sow seed 8 to 10 weeks before the first expected fall frost. Plant them 1 inch apart, thinning to 4 to 5 inches apart. Keep the soil evenly moist until germination, which only takes a few days. Continue to irrigate regularly, giving plants 1 to 2 inches of water per week. If allowed to go to seed, the plant will produce pointy pods, which are also edible.

PULLING PEPPERY ROOTS

Round black Spanish radishes can be harvested at any size — from Ping Pong ball to softball — but the peppery bite will be more subtle in the young roots. The long-rooted type is best harvested when it reaches the expected "days to maturity" and the taproots have filled out.

These radishes can be left in the garden, under mulch, for cold-season harvesting in Zones 4 to 7. They can also be harvested, topped, and stored in the refrigerator in a plastic bag for at least a month. When stored (in the ground or in the fridge), the sharpness of the raw flesh decreases.

The zingy flavor of these radishes can be tempered with a bit of cooking: sauté in butter until tender; or slice them into thin chips, rub them with olive oil, and roast them in the oven until crisp. If you can take the heat, I dare you to try them raw, grating or cutting the roots into matchsticks for salads. Pair them with sweeter foods like apples and carrots, mixing all three and tossing with a light vinaigrette. Or thinly slice and salt a few roots, and enjoy with a mug of your favorite brew.

And don't forget the foliage! The vigorous, upright leaves are edible and nutritious. They can be chopped raw for salads or wilted with garlic and olive oil in a pan for a zippy side dish.

BLACK SPANISH RADISH VARIETIES

'NERO TONDO' (55–60 days). This is an improved strain that is reliable and resistant to bolting. It's best planted for a fall crop, and it yields a uniform harvest of round black roots.

'LONG BLACK SPANISH' (70–80 days). This rare heirloom has long, tapered roots that grow 8 to 10 inches long.

WHY GROW ORDINARY RADISHES?

Rat-tailed radish

GROWING RADISHES IS QUITE ADDICTIVE!
I plant at least a dozen different varieties from spring through late summer — but only a little of each type, so that we don't have a glut at any one time. Over-mature radishes don't hold their quality well and can split, become woody, or bolt if left in the ground too long. Other than that though, radishes are very easy to grow! Here are a few of my favorite varieties.

'GERMAN BEER' (55 days). If planted in August, these snappy white radishes will be ready just in time for Oktoberfest. They are traditionally sliced into thin spirals, salted, and served in a pile beside a tankard of beer and fresh-baked pretzels. An irresistible nibble! The roots grow big, like a turnip — up to 3 inches wide and 8 inches long. The flesh is bright white, with a crisp texture and spicy flavor. The foliage is also vigorous and takes up more space than short-season radishes like 'Cherry Belle'. 'German Beer' radishes can also be pickled or sliced thin for sandwiches.

'CINCINNATI MARKET' (35 days). These are so much fun to grow! The kids think they look like small, slender carrots, and they love the deep reddish pink color of the skin. 'Cincinnati Market' is a rather scarce variety and forms straight, tapered roots that usually grow about 6 inches long. The color is only skin deep, however, as the crisp flesh is bright white. The seeds can be planted very close together — just an inch apart — and will yield their mildly spicy roots in about 5 weeks.

'CHINA ROSE' (55 days). This popular heirloom is grown as a winter radish, with the harvest beginning as the daylight diminishes in mid to late autumn. It's remarkable for its rose pink skin and squat, cylindrical shape. The roots will grow 1½ to 2 inches in diameter and 6 to 8 inches long. The flesh is bright white with a pungent sweetness that we love in salads and stir-fries. This is an excellent choice for a fall and winter garden, with the flavor growing sweeter as the mercury plunges. Mulch it or grow it in cold frames. Sow thickly in a shallow container or tray and keep moist. The pinkish green sprouts will be ready to eat in just a few days.

'China Rose'

RAT-TAILED RADISH (45–50 days). Tell your friends you're growing a radish for its seedpods and wait to see their puzzled expressions! Rat-tailed radish is truly a unique vegetable — with an unfortunate name. It's been selected over the centuries for its heavy production of tender pods, not for its roots. The plants can grow up to 4 feet tall and are heavily branched with dozens of pods per plant. Sow in spring, summer, and fall. Because its energy goes into flower and pod production, not root growth, it's a good idea to stake the plants once they reach 2 feet tall. They become top heavy very quickly and are susceptible to toppling over in wind or a rainstorm. Rat-tailed radish is a dual-purpose crop — it attracts and supports pollinating and beneficial insects with pretty flowers that range in color from white to pink. As the flowers fade, the slender pods take center stage. The smooth pods look a bit like small green beans, but the flavor is all radish: peppery and crunchy. Toss them in salads or add them to stir-fries, curries, sautés, or pickled mixtures.

'SWEET BABY' (40–45 days). An All-America Selections winner, 'Sweet Baby' is a recent introduction with short, oblong roots that grow just 3 inches long and look much like a small potato. Plus, the squat roots have unusual violet-purple skin and crisp, white flesh that is streaked with purple. Like most radishes, 'Sweet Baby' is very easy to grow and fast to mature; it's ready just 6 weeks from seeding. It can also be grown in a large pot that is at least 10 inches deep. Water often for the highest-quality roots.

don't forget the foliage!

If you're only eating the roots of your radishes, you're missing out! Radish leaves are delicious and taste very much like mustard greens: peppery and bright. Harvest the leaves from your favorite varieties, or plant those specifically bred for leaf production. Leaf radishes are fast growing and yield high-quality foliage that is less hairy (a common complaint about radish leaves).

Radish leaves can be eaten at any stage: as a sprout, microgreen, baby leaf, or full-size plant. For baby leaf and mature crops, sow the seed in a sunny garden bed a week or two before the last expected spring frost and again in late summer for fall harvesting. The plants thrive in the cool weather and mature in just 3 to 5 weeks. If you're short on space, try growing radish leaves in a pot or window box. Just be sure to water them often, as container-grown plants need regular moisture for optimum flavor and tenderness.

We nibble on the young leaves raw, but we prefer to lightly cook the mature plants. The quickest way to enjoy them is to sauté a bunch with some olive oil and chopped garlic. After just a few minutes, the greens wilt into a tasty side dish. You can also chop the leaves and add handfuls to soups, quiche, stir-fries, and curries.

RADISH LEAF VARIETIES

'SAISAI' forms vigorous rosettes that grow up to a foot tall. The lush green leaves are virtually hairless and can be eaten fresh, cooked, or turned into a refreshing kimchi.

'SAISAI PURPLE' has all the great characteristics of 'Saisai', but the

'Saisai Purple'

stems are deep purple-red. Harvest baby leaves for mixed salads, or let them mature for cooked dishes.

'HONG VIT' is a popular variety with red stems and tender, almost hairless leaves. Grow it as a microgreen or pick the baby leaves just 3 weeks after seeding. It can also be grown for a fall and winter crop in cold frames; seed densely in early autumn.

growing great radishes

> Like most root crops, radishes grow best when direct-seeded in the garden. They prefer full sun but can also be grown in partial shade, especially in Zone 7 or warmer. The soil should be well drained and fertile; I like to work in about an inch of compost or aged manure before planting.

> Radishes can be planted in pots, but the container should be large enough to accommodate the size of the root. For this reason, long-rooted types like daikon are best grown in the garden.

> Winter radishes are planted in mid to late summer for fall and winter harvest. When grown in the spring, they have a tendency to bolt when spring shifts to summer. Large-rooted types need deep, loose soil. If grown in compacted or dense soil, the roots can fork or become otherwise malformed. Raised beds are preferred.

> Radish seeds are very small, and it's easy to plant too many. Try to space the seeds of small varieties ½ inch apart, thinning to 2 inches. Larger-growing types can be seeded every 2 inches and thinned to 4 to 8 inches, depending on the mature root size. Eat those yummy thinnings as baby greens.

> Water regularly if there has been no rain. For the quick-growing spring radishes, fertilizer isn't needed. For slower-growing winter radishes, give them a boost halfway through their growth by watering in a balanced liquid organic fertilizer or fish emulsion.

> Pay attention to the "days to maturity" line on the seed packet; this will be your guide to harvesting. Usually, radishes push themselves out of the soil as they near maturity, but if you're not sure, pull one to see. There's nothing like a taste test while standing in the garden.

like turnips?

grow unusual varieties

IT'S SAD TO SAY IT, but this member of the cabbage family is often an afterthought in the veggie plot. I don't know many people who get excited about the thought of growing turnips, but let's change that! Say it with me: "We love turnips! We love turnips!"

As is true for many vegetables, seeking out unusual, global, or heirloom varieties makes this humble plant so much more interesting. In the turnip family, there's quite a range of root sizes, shapes, and colors, but no matter the appearance, most have a mild, sweet flavor that is enhanced when the plants are grown in the cool temperatures of autumn. As with radishes and beets, the foliage of turnips is edible. For more information on turnip greens, see page 94.

When I was a kid, we ate turnips on a fairly regular basis. Except that we weren't really eating turnips; we were eating rutabagas! It wasn't until I was a teenager poring through spring seed catalogs that I discovered the difference. Curious, I ordered several varieties of turnips and was surprised how easy they were to grow, and how delicious they tasted. Ever since, I've been a bit of a turnip nerd and continue to seek out heirloom and unusual varieties like 'Orange Jelly', 'Hinona Kabu', or 'Hidabeni'.

'HINONA KABU' (45–50 days). Hey market gardeners, are you listening? The unique bicolored, carrot-shaped roots of 'Hinona Kabu' are a sure-fire seller at farmers' markets. Bunch 'em up and watch them disappear off your table. This Japanese variety has slender 1½-inch-wide taproots that

'Orange Jelly'

'Milan White'

quality of our garden crops persisting into December with just a mini hoop tunnel for protection. The deep green, hairless leaves of 'Hakurei' are a favorite of my husband and mother-in-law. They have a mild mustardy flavor that makes a wonderful salad. They can be lightly sautéed and tossed into just-cooked pasta or added to a stir-fry in the last minute or two of cooking.

'ORANGE JELLY' (45 days). Once I heard that name, I couldn't resist trying this heirloom variety. It's also called 'Golden Ball' or by its French name 'Boule D'or', but I'll stick to 'Orange Jelly', thank you very much. The rounded roots have an orange-gold skin with straw-colored flesh and can grow 4 to 5 inches across. The flavor is exceptional; mild and sweet, with the best-tasting roots coming from a fall harvest. It's been called the turnip for people who don't like turnips.

'DES VERTUS MARTEAU' (45–50 days). This French heirloom isn't going to win any beauty contests, but it might win a taste test. The odd-looking roots are barrel shaped, growing 5 to 6 inches long and 2 inches across. The bottoms of the roots are a bit fatter than the tops, giving them a slight pear shape. The skin and flesh are white with a pleasing crunch and a mild sugary sweetness. If allowed to overmature, they have a tendency to form hollow centers.

'HIDABENI' (45 days). "What's wrong with those turnips?" asked my kids, pointing to the handful of 'Hidabeni' turnips I had just picked. They were curious about the unusual flattened shape of the roots, which kind of look like cipollini onions. "Nothing," I said, "They're supposed to look like that." They weren't convinced, but once we tried them, the funny shape wasn't mentioned again. This is a beautiful root with bright red skin and crisp, white flesh, which is

can grow as long as 12 inches long. Those striking roots are white, but they have purple-red shoulders. This is a variety that can be eaten raw or cooked, but in Japan it's typically pickled. Because they grow long, give them deep, loose soil or a raised bed to ensure long, straight roots.

'HAKUREI' (35 days). This is the variety that introduced me to the wonder of turnips. It's a Japanese cultivar that forms beautiful white, round, Ping-Pong-ball–size roots that are sweet and mild. It's not often you can slice up a raw vegetable and have kids say, "Yum!" It's that good. It also has excellent cold tolerance, with the sometimes streaked with a bit of the red. We don't bother to peel that brilliant skin, which just adds to the beauty of a veggie tray. This would also be a good pickling turnip, adding its bold hue to the finished pickles.

'MILAN WHITE' (35–45 days). I like to call this by its Italian name, 'Bianca Piatta Quarantina', which is so much fun to say! This heirloom has pure white roots with a round-flattened shape. It's quick to grow and tolerant of cold weather. These can be sown in a cold frame in late winter for an extra-early harvest of tender-crispy roots. For the best taste, pick when the roots are 2 to 4 inches across.

'PETROWSKI' (35 days). If you like sweet turnips, try 'Petrowski', a Polish heirloom with round, slightly flattened roots. The roots grow 2 to 3½ inches wide and are golden yellow inside and outside. The flavor is sweet with a bright turnip flavor, and the plants are ready to pull in just 5 weeks. Because it's so quick growing, it makes a good choice for interplanting. We tuck it between slower-growing crops like tomatoes, kale, and cabbages. By the time the long-season crops need the space, 'Petrowski' is ready to harvest.

'Petrowski'

growing great turnips

> Plant in early spring, 2 to 3 weeks before the last expected frost (or even earlier, if you have space in your cold frames). Turnips like a sunny site with decent, well-drained soil, though in Zone 7 and warmer, they do well in partial shade.

> Work in some compost or rotted manure before planting and sow the seeds 1 inch apart. Thin to 3 inches as they grow, using the thinnings as a baby green or as an edible garnish.

> When growing in containers, choose one that's at least 15 inches wide and 10 inches deep (or deeper, if growing long-rooted varieties). Water garden and container crops regularly to ensure crisp, mild-flavored roots.

> Turnips are ready to harvest just 5 or 6 weeks from sowing. The roots can be harvested when quite tiny and stir-fried whole with the leaves still attached. A perfect mouthful! We start picking in earnest when the roots are about 1½ inches wide, trying to take every second plant so that the remaining roots continue to size up.

> Eat your greens! We like to slice the tops into salads, drizzling with olive oil, lemon juice, and salt. Delicious, with a touch of mustardy zing.

> To store turnips, chop off the tops (leaving them will draw energy from the roots) and place the unwashed roots in a plastic bag. They can last from weeks to months when stored in the fridge or a root cellar.

like bulb onions?

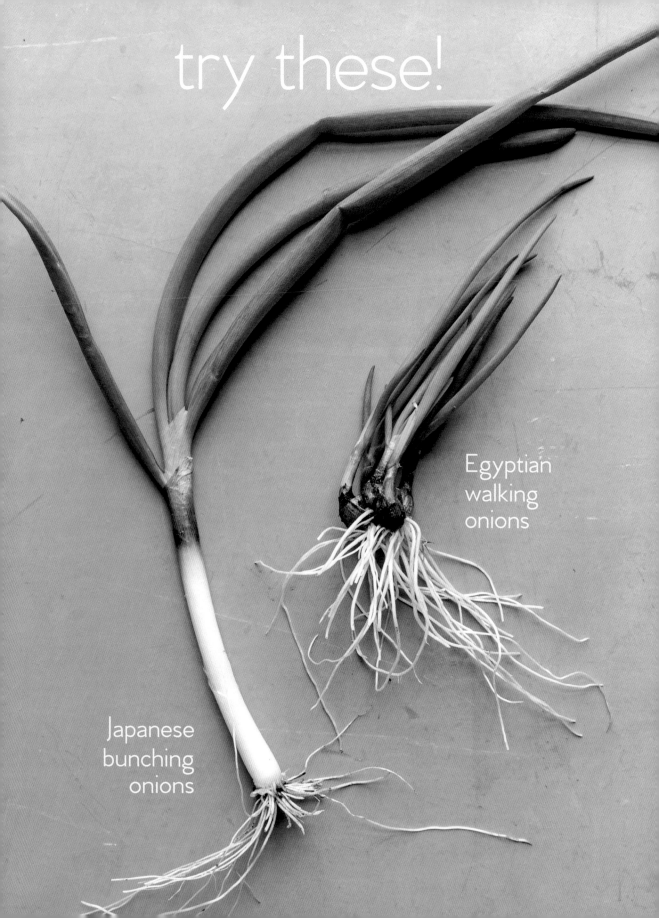

try these!

Egyptian
walking
onions

Japanese
bunching
onions

O nions are among the most widely used vegetables, playing a supporting role to countless recipes. However, I used to think that growing onions in our kitchen garden was a waste of space, because they're so cheap at the supermarket and farmers' market. Then I fell in love with the incredible variety of heirloom and Asian varieties. I found that I just couldn't do without these culinary treasures.

Unfortunately, as with many unusual crops, if you want them, you're probably going to have to grow them yourself. I happen upon a few unique and heirloom onions at the farmers' market from time to time, but generally, they aren't easy to source. So I now make space in our garden beds for favorites like 'Borettana' cipollini and 'Red Beard' bunching onion. They're easy-to-grow, low-maintenance crops that are bothered by few pests and diseases. Plus, bunching onions can be stored for months! Green onions and scallions can't.

Japanese Bunching Onions

MY INTRODUCTION TO Japanese bunching onions was 'Evergreen Hardy White', a popular cold-hardy variety that I tested in my late-fall and winter cold frames. It proved to be a spectacular onion, with vigorous green tops and flavorful white stems, and I began to seek out other cultivars of Japanese bunching onions.

This type of onion can be grown as an annual or left in place to overwinter and form a sizable perennial clump. They don't develop bulbs, like bulbing onions, but rather form ½- to ¾-inch-thick stems with vigorous green tops. Established plants are also ornamental, and in summer produce round white flowers that attract pollinators and beneficial insects.

Japanese bunching onions adapt to a wide range of growing conditions but do best when planted in full sun and organic, well-drained soil. If space in the vegetable garden is short, try planting them in the perennial border, edible forest, or herb beds. If allowed to naturalize, the plants will grow 2 to 3 feet tall with upright, spiky foliage.

To grow as an annual crop, direct seed in early spring for late-spring and early-summer harvests. Sow seed again in late summer for fall harvesting. Autumn seedings in cold frames or poly tunnels can be harvested from early to late winter. You can also propagate by dividing mature clumps for replanting and sharing.

It's important to keep newly planted seeds consistently watered to ensure good germination. As well, remove weeds as they appear. Young Japanese bunching onions are rather delicate looking in their first few weeks and won't compete well against weeds. Established plants are better suited to challenge weeds. They're also quite drought tolerant.

You can harvest the hollow green stems as scallions anytime from early spring through late autumn. Our kids love them sliced into miso or egg drop soup, but we also use them in salads, stir-fries, dips, egg dishes, and fried rice and to top baked potatoes and so on.

BEST BUNCHING ONIONS

'RED BEARD' (50–60 days). We love the striking purple-red stalks of this Japanese bunching onion, which is ready just 2 months from seeding. These can grow quite tall — up to 2 feet — with dense green tops and firm, slender stalks that are 5 to 10 inches long. Flavor is mild.

'HE SHI KO' (75–80 days). This is an outstanding Japanese bunching onion that has deep green tubular leaves that grow about a foot tall. They won't form bulbs, but the bright white bottoms of the stems are dense and aromatic, growing ½ to ¾ inch across. I first grew this variety in hopes that it would be winter hardy in our cold frames; it was, and we now have these year-round — in the garden and cold frames.

'ISHIKURA IMPROVED' (60–70 days). We love this traditional Japanese scallion, which can grow very tall, up to 2 feet, with long, slender white stalks. If planted early, the stems can grow ¾ to 1 inch in diameter, almost like a small leek, and with a similar sweet flavor. To produce the longest white stems, hill up the plants with soil a few weeks before harvesting.

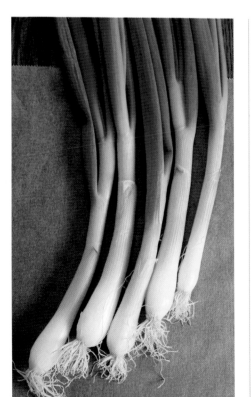

Many supermarket scallions are actually varieties of Japanese bunching onions. If you buy a bunch that has roots still attached, you can plant the rooted stubs in the garden for a fresh crop!

THE DETAILS

A.K.A.: Spring onion, Welsh onion, negi, *Allium fistulosum*

DAYS TO MATURITY: Perennial in Zones 4–9

HAILS FROM: China

VARIETIES TO TRY: 'Red Beard', 'He Shi Ko', 'Ishikura Improved'

Egyptian Walking Onions

THE DETAILS

A.K.A.: Tree onion, walking onion, *Allium cepa* var. *proliferum*

DAYS TO MATURITY: Perennial in Zones 5–9

HAILS FROM: Asia

VARIETIES TO TRY: None

ALSO CALLED TREE ONION, this funny fellow will "walk" around your garden by top-setting small bulbils that eventually fall to the ground and sprout, beginning the process again. Egyptian walking onions are a cross between bulbing onions and bunching onions; they form hardy perennial plants that yield tender green onions for much of the year. They do form bulbs at the bottom of the plant, but it's those quirky clusters of bulbils that make this a walking onion.

Because of its tendency to roam, Egyptian walking onions are popular among permaculturists, who use it in forest gardens and other plantings. They're a low-maintenance crop, needing little from the gardener except a place to wander.

LET 'EM WALK

Egyptian walking onions can be grown from divisions from an established patch or from top sets planted in the spring or fall. If you have a choice, plant in autumn to give the plants a head start on growth. To plant, separate the top sets into individual bulbs, planting each one about 2 inches deep and 6 to 8 inches apart. Depending on your climate and the growing year, they may not produce top sets their first year. Be patient; it won't take long to establish a dense crop of Egyptian walking onions.

To control the spread of the plants, remove any top sets that have fallen to the ground in mid-autumn. They can be used in the kitchen, shared among friends, or replanted in a different location.

Harvesting of the vigorous greens begins in very early spring, a few weeks after the snow melts, and continues through late autumn — longer in milder climates. The main bulb can also be harvested in autumn, but we prefer the bulbils that form at the top of woody stalks in summer. By early autumn, the weight of the top set pushes the stalk down to the ground, where it will root and continue the "walking" cycle. We harvest the bulbils for use as baby onions, adding them to countless dishes — even slipping them on skewers for shish kebab — but they can also be used for pickling and preserving.

growing great onions

> Growing onions from seed takes a long time, with seeds started indoors in late winter to get a jump on the season. But starting with seeds gives you access to the widest selection of varieties.

> Onions are daylight sensitive and need a certain amount of daylight in order to start forming bulbs, so be sure to choose the type that's right for your region: long day (14–16 hours of daylight), short day (10–12 hours of daylight), or day-neutral (12–14 hours of daylight).

> Onion "sets" — small onions that were planted densely and harvested late the season before — are sold in garden centers each spring. Growing onions from sets is easy, cheap, and convenient and will yield a harvest that is usually earlier than growing from seed. The downside is that only a few varieties are offered as sets.

> To seed your own onions, sow them indoors in flats about 10 weeks before the last expected spring frost. As the seedlings grow, scissor trim to remove the tiny black seed husks, which often don't fall off on their own and can weigh down the young shoots. Every week or so, I continue to use scissors to trim the seedlings back to about 3 inches. This encourages them to thicken up and prevents legginess.

> About 2 weeks before the last expected frost date, start to harden off the seedlings. They can go in the garden when the night temperature is in the 46 to 52°F (8 to 11°C) range. Prolonged exposure to cold temperatures can induce bolting, but you can set them out earlier in beds covered with mini hoop tunnels.

> Grow onions in full sun and well-drained, rich soil. Amend the garden bed with several inches of compost or rotted manure before planting, as well as a balanced organic fertilizer. Space onion sets or seedlings 5 to 6 inches apart.

> Nonbulbing scallions can be direct-seeded in the open garden a few weeks before the last expected frost and spaced just an inch apart. I carefully sprinkle the seeds over a 1-square-foot patch of garden; of course, they eventually need to be thinned out, and we also eat those tender, tiny thinnings.

> As the plants grow, irrigate weekly with 1 to 2 inches of water if there has been no soaking rain. Reduce watering in the weeks before harvest, as too much water can dilute the onion flavor.

> Onions don't produce a dense canopy of foliage to shade the soil and discourage weeds, and therefore you will need to pull weeds as they appear.

> In late summer, sow a fresh seeding of scallions into cold frames. Certain varieties, like 'Evergreen Hardy White', are very cold tolerant and offer a high-quality crop for winter harvesting.

> Scallions are quick to mature, ready in 60 to 80 days. For the sweetest, mildest scallions, plan to harvest when the plants are at their flavor peak: about 10 to 12 weeks old. We succession plant a square foot of scallions every month to ensure a long season of top-quality plants.

> Bulbing onions need a long season — often up to 120 days, depending on the variety. You can pull them as soon as they reach a harvestable size. For a storage crop, you'll need to let them mature in ground. You know they're just about ready to pull when most of their tops have flopped over and begin to yellow. Leave them in the ground for an additional 10 to 14 days to finish maturing.

> Harvest bulb onions on a sunny, mild day, leaving the onions to lie on the soil for a few hours to dry out the roots. If the weather is cool, this might take a few days. In hot climates, the roots will dry up in a few hours. Avoid pulling onions in wet weather, which can reduce their storage quality.

> Bring onions indoors or to a sheltered, well-ventilated spot to cure. Curing can take 2 to 3 weeks. Once fully cured, the onions should be stored in mesh bags in a root cellar or cool storage.

WHY GROW ORDINARY BULB ONIONS?

'RED OF FLORENCE' (LONG DAY). This famous Italian heirloom was my first foray into seed-grown onions, and I've grown it every year since. It's also called 'Lunga di Firenze' and 'Italian Red Torpedo', likely for its quirky slender bulbs and bright red skin. The bulbs grow up to 4 inches in length, but just 1½ to 2 inches across. The flavor is remarkably sweet, and we like them sliced thinly in arugula salad or sprinkled on top of homemade pizza. Properly cured, the bulbs will last for months in storage.

'BORETTANA' CIPOLLINI (LONG DAY). I'm an onion hoarder. When our beautiful red-and-yellow cipollini onions have been harvested, cured, and stored, I still resist using them because I just love them so much. I know it makes no sense, but they have such attractive flattened bulbs and meltingly sweet flavor that I just want them to last as long as possible. 'Borettana' is one of my favorites; the compact, UFO-shaped bulbs grow just 2 to 3 inches wide and 1 inch deep, with golden brown skin. They can be stored for up to 5 months.

'RED MARBLE' CIPOLLINI (LONG DAY). Onion lovers will adore this unique variety that has bulbs the same shape and size as 'Borettana' but in a rich red color. These are often planted just 2 inches apart to produce small, compact bulbs, but they can be spaced farther apart to yield larger onions. The bulbs are extremely firm and also store well.

'RED BARON' (LONG DAY). For several years, I grew this unusual variety as a scallion, enjoying the dark purple-red stalks and leafy greens. It wasn't until I neglected to harvest them in a timely manner that I discovered it wasn't a nonbulbing scallion but rather a bulbing onion with attractive small to medium-size bulbs that are wonderfully mild in salads, salsa, and other fresh dishes. The small bulbs can also be pickled.

'PURPLETTE' (SHORT DAY). Because of my northern location, most of the bulbing onions I grow are long-day types. However, I've had good luck with 'Purplette', a short-day onion that is quick and easy to grow for flavorful baby bulbs. The small bulbs are ridiculously pretty with amethyst-purple skin and can be harvested as bunching onions or as small pearl onions, or allowed to grow to Ping-Pong-ball–size bulbs. Great mild flavor in salads and raw dishes. With cooking, the color softens to pink.

'RED CREOLE' (SHORT DAY). This is another good pick for southern gardeners, who will appreciate the purple-pink skin and white interiors of this heirloom variety. The flavor is more spicy than sweet, and the bulbs get up to 4 inches across. With proper storage, they will last up to 5 months.

'Red Marble'

'Red Baron'

'Red of Florence'

like parsnips?
try hamburg parsley!

HAMBURG PARSLEY IS UNCOMMON enough that no one ever seems to know what it is when I show off its squat, white roots to garden visitors. But it's not hard to find in catalogs; seed for varieties like 'Arat' and 'Hamburg Half-Long' are available from several sources.

In addition to being delicious, it also matures relatively early; roots are ready to harvest in a mere 75 to 85 days, compared to the 110 to 120 days needed to mature parsnips. The white taproots do resemble small parsnips or white carrots growing up to 6 inches long and 2 inches wide at the shoulder. Their flavor hints of the sweetness of parsnips and carrots, but to me it's more parsley-celery, lacking the earthy quality of parsnips.

SLOW AND STEADY

Hamburg parsley needs full sun and soil that is fertile and loose. Raised beds are ideal. It's grown like a carrot: direct-seeded in early spring, about 2 to 3 weeks before the last expected frost. Space the seeds 1 inch apart, thinning to 6 inches once the seedlings are growing well. As with parsnips, germination is slow, so be patient and keep the seedbed evenly moist until the plants emerge in about 3 weeks. As

the plants grow, continue to water weekly if rain is scarce, and mulch with straw or shredded leaves to keep soil cool and moist. If grown in dry soil, the roots are prone to forking.

Hamburg parsley is a biennial. If you're growing an heirloom variety like 'Hamburg Half-Long', you can allow some of the plants to overwinter and produce seeds for future harvests.

SNIPPING TOPS, PULLING UP ROOTS

This is a "two for one" veggie, with the harvest of the parsley-flavored tops taking place over the summer and into autumn. Modestly harvest from the vigorous tops as they grow, but don't take too much from each plant, as you don't want to delay the growth of the roots. Use the foliage as you would Italian parsley.

Start pulling roots around 75 days from seeding. If they're still quite small, wait a few more weeks. They're great raw — snappy and crisp — but they also add a depth of flavor to soups and stews and a medley of roasted root vegetables. We also like to cube them and add a few handfuls to boiling potatoes, mashing the whole pot together when fork-tender.

THE DETAILS

A.K.A.: Root parsley, turnip-rooted parsley, Wurzelpetersilie (in Germany), *Petroselinum crispum* var. *tuberosum*

DAYS TO MATURITY: 75–85 days

HAILS FROM: Germany

VARIETIES TO TRY: 'Arat', 'Hamburg Half-Long'

nine
global herbs
you need
to know

For me, the journey into gardening began with *The Harrowsmith Illustrated Book of Herbs* by Patrick Lima. I was just sixteen years old, but was instantly inspired to try my hand at growing herbs. I started with common types like curly parsley, oregano, thyme, and basil, but as they grew and we were able to harvest and use them in our cooking, I became more adventurous. Soon, I was planting chamomile, lemongrass, lovage, and hyssop and discovering just how easy they were to grow.

I've never lost my love of herb gardening and continue to seek out unusual, historic, or global herbs like papalo, perilla, and edible chrysanthemum. Often, it's for practicality. Cilantro, for example, is a common herb, but one that tends to bolt with frustrating rapidity in the garden.

Yet papalo and Vietnamese coriander both make satisfying cilantro substitutes and remain vigorous all summer long. Whatever your reasons for trying new herbs, I think you'll discover that the following nine make worthwhile and beautiful garden plants.

TRY THIS!
Syrian Oregano

THE DETAILS

A.K.A.: *Origanum syriacum*

DAYS TO MATURITY: Perennial in Zones 7–10

HAILS FROM: Middle East to Mediterranean region

VARIETIES TO TRY: None

SEVERAL DAYS A WEEK, we start our morning with man'ouche, a homemade Lebanese flatbread that is topped with an aromatic mixture called za'atar. Za'atar is a blend of spices, which includes dried Syrian oregano, toasted sesame seeds, sumac, and salt. This is mixed with olive oil to make a slurry and then spread over a round of unbaked dough, similar to a pizza dough. Within minutes of putting the man'ouche in the oven, the entire house smells heavenly, and soon we are all sitting down to an authentic Lebanese breakfast.

Some may argue that Syrian oregano isn't the true spice used in za'atar. It's true that, depending where you are in the world, dozens of plants, often in the oregano, thyme or savory families are called za'atar. In my husband's home village in Lebanon, *Thymbra spicata* or summer savory most often used to make za'atar. However, I've found it very difficult to source seed or plants for *T. spicata*, and the easier-to-find Syrian oregano makes an outstanding substitute.

SUNNY AND DRY

In its native Mediterranean habitat, Syrian oregano can grow up to 3 feet tall. In my garden, it reaches just 15 to 18 inches and has a loose, spreading habit. The small silvery green leaves are very ornamental and soft to touch. Because I want our plants to get as large as possible in our short growing season, I give them a head start indoors,

sowing the seed in mid to late March, about 8 weeks before the last expected frost. The small seedlings go into the garden when the danger of frost has passed. They thrive in full sun and well-drained soil and are quite drought tolerant. They also seem immune to pests and disease, at least in my climate.

Syrian oregano is a perfect pot plant, growing happily in window boxes or planters. If our summer is warm enough, the plants will flower — tiny white blooms that attract pollinators and beneficial bugs. Frequent harvesting will encourage bushy growth. Place it where the foliage can be rubbed to release the rich scent. Potted plants can be moved indoors for winter harvesting; just give them a sunny window away from drafts.

DRYING FOR ZA'ATAR

To get your Syrian oregano ready to make za'atar, you'll need to dry the leaves. Cut 6- to 10-inch-long branches, gathering them into small bundles. Hang these upside down in a well-ventilated, airy location, but out of direct sunlight. Once dry, remove the leaves from the stems and crumble. Store the dried herb in a jar. We mainly use za'atar to make man'ouche, but you can also use it in meat marinades, spread it on croissants just before baking, or sprinkle it on pita chips before you toast them and dip them in hummus.

My mother-in-law likes to pickle the fresh leafy stems of Syrian oregano, which she serves with her homemade falafel. There are many ways to enjoy this savory herb. Don't be shy about experimenting with it in your own garden.

Two strains of
Syrian oregano

Summer
savory

Perilla

MY INTRODUCTION TO THIS CLASSIC Asian herb came from two seed packets a friend brought back from Hong Kong about a decade ago. One packet said "green perilla" and the other "purple perilla," but that was the extent of the English writing on the envelopes, so I had no idea what these mystery plants were or how to grow them.

With a little research, I soon learned that perilla is a member of the mint family.

It has the typical square stem of a mint, but its leaves are large and teardrop-shaped, with sharp serration along the edge. The leaves can be flat or crinkly, depending on the variety, and in good soil, they can grow as big as your palm.

The plants, and in particular the purple ones, are highly ornamental. The foliage of the green type is bright green on top but purple underneath. Purple perilla leaves are burgundy-purple, top and bottom, and make a striking bedding or container plant. As for flavor, it was hard to place, at first: the green perilla tasted a bit like mint with notes of basil and even cinnamon; the purple type had a hint of anise.

That first summer, the perilla thrived and we brought a bouquet of the leaves to the chef at our favorite sushi restaurant. He was thrilled by the gift, and said that perilla is often used for wrapping sushi, but that he also likes to dip the leaves in tempura and flash-fry them. The shoots and leaves can be pickled or turned into a gourmet pesto. The red variety is used in pickled ginger to give it that characteristic pink hue. We add the leaves to our homemade sushi, but we also sliver them and toss them into salads, iced tea, and lemonade, as well as in stir-fries during the last moments of cooking. In winter, perilla can be grown as a microgreen by seeding it thickly under grow lights.

BEWARE: SELF-SEEDER!
Like amaranth and magenta spreen, perilla is an enthusiastic self-seeder and

is considered an exotic invasive in areas where it has spilled into natural areas. Therefore, gardener beware! If perilla is invasive in your region, grow it responsibly: pull the plants before they set seed. Perilla is an annual plant and does not spread by rhizomes like its mint cousins, so its spread can be effectively controlled by simple garden maintenance.

For a plant that can be invasive, it's a bit ironic that it can be hard to germinate. I initially tried starting perilla indoors, under my grow lights, but the germination was spotty, sometimes nonexistent. The key is to buy fresh seed and sow it on the soil surface. The seeds need light to germinate, so just press them into the potting soil and keep them moist until germination. I start perilla in cell packs, sowing 3 to 4 seeds per cell, and scissor thin them to the strongest

seedling when the first true leaves emerge. Perilla can also be direct sown in the garden. Sow the seed a week or two before the last expected spring frost. Again, sprinkle the seeds on premoistened soil and gently press down to encourage good soil-to-seed contact. The plants should be thinned to a foot apart.

Perilla will grow 1½ to 3 feet tall. We pinch our plants back quite often, so they stay under 2 feet. Pinching also encourages heavy branching and will increase your harvest of foliage. Once established, perilla is relatively drought tolerant and resistant to insects and diseases. Water weekly if there hasn't been a soaking rain. Once the plants grow together, they'll form a dense canopy that shades the soil and reduces the need to water.

THE DETAILS

A.K.A.: Shiso, Japanese basil, beefsteak plant, sesame leaves (although it's not related to sesame), *Perilla frutescens* var. *crispa*

DAYS TO MATURITY: 70–80 days

HAILS FROM: India to Southeast Asia

VARIETIES TO TRY: 'Hojiso', Korean perilla

TRY THIS!
Mitsuba

THE DETAILS

A.K.A.: Japanese parsley, white chervil, *Cryptotaenia japonica*

DAYS TO MATURITY: Perennial in Zones 4–9

HAILS FROM: East Asia

VARIETIES TO TRY: *Cryptotaenia japonica* var. *atropurpurea* is a purple form; it's very ornamental!

MITSUBA LOOKS A LOT LIKE Italian parsley: deep green trilobed leaves held atop long, slender stalks. The flavor is bright and strong and seems to combine parsley with celery and a hint of chervil. (It should come as no surprise, then, that it's also called Japanese parsley or white chervil.) Unlike the annual leaf celery and the biennial Italian parsley, mitsuba is a hardy perennial, thriving in Zones 4 to 9.

A SHADE-LOVING SELF-SOWER

It's important to note that like perilla, mitsuba will self-seed prolifically and should therefore be planted in a spot where it

won't wander into uncultivated areas. I like to grow it in pots or planters on my deck or patio, where self-seeding isn't an issue. Garden-grown mitsuba can be controlled by trimming off the tiny white blooms when they appear, but that's a big job (and one that will need to be repeated every year), so planting in pots makes sense. We also tuck it into our early-autumn cold frames, which allows us to enjoy a winter-long harvest of the flavorful leaves. We pinch the flowers as they appear to prevent this self-sower from taking over our frames!

This culinary herb prefers shade over sun and is perfect for a woodland setting, forest garden, or other shady nook. It can grow several feet tall, but frequent harvesting keeps the plant's height to about 10 to 12 inches. Rich soil will encourage a continual supply of fresh growth, so dig in some compost before planting. Direct seed or start indoors; the main harvest will begin about 2 months from seeding. Space plants 1 foot apart, or just 6 inches apart if you intend to harvest the young shoots.

To harvest, you can clip off as much as you need — it's got a powerful flavor, so err on the side of "less is more" — or you can give it a haircut a few inches above the crown, treating it as a cut-and-come-again crop. With a little fish emulsion watered into the stubs, it will quickly regrow.

The leaves and stems of mitsuba are used both raw and cooked, but should be added only in the last few minutes of cooking time; the flavor can turn bitter when the foliage is overcooked. Use fresh leaves and stems in salads or to top soups (like miso), rice, meat dishes, stir-fries, noodles, or sashimi. It can also be pickled or used as an appealing garnish.

TRY THIS!
Thai Basil

IN MY NAIVETÉ, the first time I tried Thai basil, I expected it to have a flavor similar to my beloved sweet basil. I was wrong! Thai basil has a flavor all its own: a spicy mix of licorice and cloves that remains strong even after cooking. I like to sliver the leaves and sprinkle them in curry and noodle dishes, but they also jazz up a simple tomato and cucumber salad.

Thai basil is highly decorative, with slender dark green leaves, burgundy-purple stems and matching burgundy-purple flower clusters that have tiny pink petals. The flower clusters are also edible; sprinkle them on salads for a pop of licorice-clove flavor.

SUN AND HEAT

As with sweet basil, Thai basil is a warm-season herb that needs full sun and plenty of heat. I start the seeds indoors in late March under my grow lights. By the time the last frost has come and gone, I'm ready to start hardening them off. Don't be in a rush to put them in the garden, though; setting the plants out too early can lead to disappointment. Simple cloches or a mini hoop tunnel over the plants will protect them when the temperature drops, but I rarely bother. It's easier to just wait until the nighttime temperature hovers around 60°F (15°C).

Thai basil plants are bushy, growing up to 2 feet tall, and they take to garden beds as well as big pots. It's also fairly low maintenance; I add compost to the garden bed before planting, and as the seedlings grow, I pinch the shoots to encourage thick growth and high leaf production (eat those wonderfully aromatic pinchings). Keep an eye out for pests like aphids, knocking any off with a hard jet of water from the hose.

In early autumn, I dig up and repot one of our Thai basil plants for the winter windowsill. Because we have short winter days, the plant eventually declines, but even still, having a plant indoors does extend the harvest into January. I also pick and dry the leaves when they're at their summer peak, and store the dried, crumbled leaves in a jar in the spice cupboard.

Award-winning 'Siam Queen' is the standard for Thai basil. It forms dense clumps of intensely flavored foliage and will continue to crop for 3 to 4 months. The blooms emerge later than other varieties, allowing the eating quality to remain high.

THE DETAILS

A.K.A.: Licorice basil, anise basil, *Ocimum basilicum* var. *thyrsiflora*

DAYS TO MATURITY: 70 days

HAILS FROM: Thought to be from Southeast Asia

VARIETIES TO TRY: 'Siam Queen', 'Thai Red Stem', 'Sweet Thai'

TRY THIS!
Chinese Chives

CHINESE CHIVES, BETTER KNOWN AS garlic chives, are fairly common in North American gardens, but with a show of hands, how many of you have actually *used* your garlic chives? Yeah, I was once guilty of this neglect. For years I enjoyed this hardy perennial only as an ornamental plant. But once I got a taste for the gentle garlic-onion flavored foliage, it became one of our essential herbs.

Garlic chives produce clumps of flat, grassy foliage that are topped with chivelike white flowers in late summer. The plants grow taller than those of regular garden chives, reaching heights of up to 2 feet. They're very low maintenance, thriving in any sunny, well-drained spot with fertile soil. The flowers are attractive to butterflies, bees, and beneficial insects, but they are also edible and can be added to soups and salads or used as a garnish.

In Asian cooking, garlic chives are typically eaten as a vegetable rather than an herb. They're great in scrambled eggs, stir-fried, or chopped into a bowl of steaming miso soup. My favorite way to use them is in my homemade vegetable dumplings — so good!

Garlic chives can be grown from seed or by divisions taken from mature plants. To keep the harvest going into winter, I cut back a clump in early fall and move it to a cold frame. Fresh shoots will soon emerge, and you can harvest all winter long.

Like regular chives, garlic chives have a tendency to self-seed, so place them where they can roam or be sure to pull out the "volunteers" each spring. You can also control reseeding by chopping off the spent flowers in late August.

If you have a few clumps of garlic chives, you might want to try blanching some for Chinese yellow chives. Traditionally, the plants are grown beneath the cover of a clay pot, but any container that omits light will do. Cut the blanched plants when they are 9 to 12 inches tall. This process results in super tender, mild-tasting, pale yellow leaves. Stir-fry the blanched leaves or use them in soups.

THE DETAILS

A.K.A.: Garlic chive, Chinese chives, Chinese leeks, *jiu cai*, *Allium tuberosum*

DAYS TO MATURITY: Perennial in Zones 4–9

HAILS FROM: Southeast Asia

VARIETIES TO TRY: 'Geisha', 'Nira'

TRY THIS!
Papalo

CILANTRO IS AN HERB you either love or hate. I'm firmly in the "love it" camp and was therefore thrilled to discover papalo, a little-known herb that has a flavor similar to cilantro. It isn't actually a member of the cilantro family, and though it does have a hint of cilantro in its flavor profile, there are other tastes there too: citrus, maybe mint, and a hint of pepperiness? It's a bit hard to pinpoint. When asked what papalo tastes like, I say, "It tastes like papalo."

In addition to being tasty, it's quite attractive, with rounded, gently scalloped blue-green leaves. The plants can grow 4 to 5 feet tall in hot climates, but when I grow it in pots on my sunny, sheltered back deck, it gets about 2 feet tall.

Papalo seed should be started indoors 6 weeks before the last expected frost. It germinates best in a warm spot, so pop the seeding tray on top of the fridge or place in a warm room. The seedlings should emerge in 7 to 10 days at 70°F (21°C). Once the plants are 4 to 5 inches tall, they can be hardened off and transplanted to the garden. At that point, the spring weather should be reliably warm and frost-free. Space the plants at least a foot apart.

As a Mexican native, papalo demands hot weather and won't bolt like cilantro does in the summer heat. Make sure to pick a site with well-drained soil, as it will decline if left with wet feet. To thicken up the plants, pinch them occasionally as they grow. If left unpinched, the plants yield slender stems prone to falling over in strong wind or heavy rain.

Papalo is used raw and should be added to dishes just before serving. Sprinkle the chopped fresh leaves directly onto your tacos, or stir them into salsa. Use a light hand; papalo leaves are packed with flavorful oils, so a little goes a long way. Start by using only one-third to one-half the amount of cilantro you would normally add to your dishes.

THE DETAILS

A.K.A.: Mexican cilantro, Bolivian coriander, or papalo-quelite, *Porophyllum ruderale* subsp. *macrocephalum*

DAYS TO MATURITY: 70 days

HAILS FROM: Central and South America

VARIETIES TO TRY: None

TRY THIS!
Edible Chrysanthemum

WHEN I FIRST SAW CHRYSANTHEMUMS listed in the "greens" section of one of my favorite seed catalogs, I thought it was a mistake. Then I read further and discovered that this plant, traditionally grown for its pretty pincushion flowers, is actually edible!

A number of varieties are available, some having broad leaves and others with finely cut, frilly leaves. Generally, the broader-leaf varieties have milder-tasting foliage, and the delicate-looking serrated types have a more pungent flavor. The plants are attractive, with silvery green leaves and sunny yellow flowers in late summer. Those flowers are also edible and can be used in teas as a garnish or added to salads.

The greens have a strong flavor that is sometimes described as astringent, slightly bitter, or even herbal. Unsure what to expect, my first taste came from a clump of baby plants that were just a few inches tall. Nibbling carefully on the raw leaf, I found it to have a slight bite, but it was a clean, green taste, and very tender in texture.

Edible chrysanthemum is easy to grow (so easy, in fact, it's considered invasive in some places — such as California). I like to grow it for a harvest of young leaves, sowing the seeds thickly in a prepared bed once the last frost has passed. They can take full sun or partial shade, with a sunny crop maturing slightly faster than those grown in less light. They also appreciate cool weather, making this a good choice for spring and fall harvesting. With the protection of a cold frame, an early-autumn seeding of edible chrysanthemum will persist into winter.

The seed is tiny, so sprinkle it lightly on the soil surface, and gently scratch it in. Once the seedlings are several inches tall, thin them to 4 to 6 inches apart, using those thinnings in stir-fries, chop suey, or mixed baby green salads. To encourage a long foliage harvest, pinch off any flower buds as they appear. The plants can grow to 3 feet tall, but I harvest most of mine long before they reach that height. Eventually, I do let a few of them flower, attracting both bees and beneficial insects.

The best-quality eating comes from young leaves and shoots that are 4 to 8 inches tall; mature foliage and stems turn bitter. Note, too, that the foliage wilts quickly after harvesting, so plan on picking just before you will be eating it. Add edible chrysanthemum to your dishes in their final moments of cooking, or stir-fry for just a few moments. If you overcook, the flavor will become bitter. Of course, you can also enjoy the leaves raw in mixed salads.

THE DETAILS

A.K.A.: Garland chrysanthemum, chop suey greens, shungiku, tong hao, *Glebionis coronaria*

DAYS TO MATURITY: 45 days

HAILS FROM: East Asia

VARIETIES TO TRY: 'Oasis', 'Komi Shuniku Salada'

TRY THIS!
Lemongrass

LEMONGRASS IS A PLANT OF MANY USES! It's a popular culinary herb in Asian cooking, imparting a wonderful citrus flavor to stir-fries. Personally, I love to prepare it as a tea (see the final paragraph, below). My good friend, Tara Nolan, often uses lemongrass in her ornamental container gardens; the spiky texture makes it a good replacement for dracaena. By switching in lemongrass, Tara ends up with the same texture but with the bonus of edible, aromatic foliage!

Lemongrass is super easy to grow. I bought a small plant in a 4-inch pot about 6 years ago from my local garden center. I moved it up to a bigger, more decorative pot, and it now goes outdoors on our sunny deck in the summer and back indoors on a sunny windowsill in the winter. You can also plant it directly into the garden and just grow it as an annual. Lemongrass likes well-drained soil and appreciates an inch or two of compost before planting. Fertilize regularly with an organic liquid fertilizer, like fish emulsion. Water potted crops often to keep flavor quality high.

In addition to buying plants from the nursery, you can purchase lemongrass at your local supermarket and plant it. Just look for stalks that still have some roots attached. When you get them home, soak them in water for an hour or so and plant them up in potting soil. They'll quickly root, and soon you'll have fresh shoots. Adventuresome gardeners may want to try growing their own lemongrass from seed; keep in mind that it will take just shy of 3 months for the plants to reach a harvestable size.

To harvest, cut the stalks at ground level. The best portion is the fleshy stalk at the bottom of the plant. Remove the outer layers of leaves to expose the tender heart. Slice and add it to soup, stir-fry, rice, curry, and a thousand other dishes. Reserve the tops of the plants for tea or meat marinades.

I love a hot, steaming cup of lemongrass tea on a cold day, and it's easy to make! Take two stalks, clipping off the root ends and discarding any dry leaves. Use a tenderizing mallet to gently bruise the stalks, then place them, green leaf tops and all, in a small pot. Add 2 cups of water and bring to a boil. Reduce the heat and simmer for 5 to 10 minutes. Pour the fragrant tea into a big mug, adding some honey or sugar, if desired.

THE DETAILS

A.K.A.: *Cymbopogon citratus*

DAYS TO MATURITY: Perennial in Zone 8 or warmer

HAILS FROM: Southeast Asia

VARIETIES TO TRY: None

TRY THIS!
Vietnamese Coriander

WHEN I WAS A TEENAGER, I became rather obsessed with growing herbs. I think I finally clued into the fact that those funny little bottles of dried green bits in my mother's spice cupboard actually came from plants, and I wanted to grow them. All of them! My love of herbs led me to Richters Herbs, a mail-order catalog in Goodwood, Ontario, which offers an incredible selection of seeds and plants. I made it my mission to order the most exotic-sounding herbs I could find, and thus I eventually discovered Vietnamese coriander.

Initially, I was attracted to the appearance of this little-known herb, which has dark green pointy foliage with V-shaped chestnut brown markings on the leaf surface. It's quite a striking combination, and one that adds interest to the collection of container-grown herbs on my deck. Once I actually *tasted* Vietnamese coriander, I became obsessed with trying to incorporate its unique, peppery-cilantro flavor into our family meals.

This member of the knotweed family will grow in full sun to partial shade and prefers moist soil. Plant it at the edge of a pond or in a boggy area, but if you don't have such a spot, you can also grow it in ordinary garden soil or containers. Just be sure to dig in plenty of compost or rotted manure before planting to boost the moisture-holding capacity of the soil. Water often to keep flavor quality high. With too little water, the leaves can become bitter.

Like lemongrass, container-grown Vietnamese coriander can be brought indoors before the first fall frost and placed in a sunny window. It can be grown from seed, but I've found seed to be difficult to source. Finding small plants at nurseries or through catalogs that specialize in herbs may be your best bet. Of course, if you can find a bundle of fresh Vietnamese coriander at your local Asian market, you can root a few stems by placing them in a jar of water for a week or two.

Young foliage offers the best-quality flavor. Shear the plants back occasionally to produce a fresh flush of leaves. I like to sprinkle the chopped leaves into salads, stir-fries, and *pho*, a Vietnamese noodle soup.

222

acknowledgments

Over the years, I've grown a lot of global, unusual, and heirloom crops. However, growing them all in one year so that they could be photographed for this book was a challenge. Luckily, we had a handful of incredible gardeners who generously shared space in their gardens for some of the crops. Huge thanks to Brenda Franklin, Craig Le-Houllier, Mark Russell, Jessi Fillmore, and Sean Saunders. Also, it was a pleasure to visit several local farmers who value global and heirloom vegetables as much as I do and were able to supply a few crops that I just didn't have space for; thank you to Camelia Frieberg of Watershed Farm and Domenic Padula and Kimm Kent of Moon Fire Farm.

The vegetables and herbs in this book were photographed as they grew in my garden or lovingly harvested and photographed in the pop-up photography studio created in my rather chaotic garage. I'd like to thank the talented photographers who turned these garden veggies into works of art: Philip Ficks of Philip Ficks Photography and his assistant Mike Pederson, and James Ingram of Jive Photographic Productions. It was a fascinating process to watch, and I fell in love with each and every photo they took.

I'd also like to thank the outstanding folks at Storey Publishing. I'm so proud to be a member of the Storey family and work with such creative and talented people. With her gift for crafting books, Carleen Madigan is the best editor in the business. She takes words and ideas and spins gold — thank you, Carleen! My heartfelt appreciation also goes to art director Carolyn Eckert for her ingenuity and artistry, which is reflected on every page in this book.

Warm thanks go out to the many gardeners on social media around the world who have supported and connected with me, but most of all, inspired me! I love seeing what you are growing and hearing about your favorite crops and varieties. I hope you enjoy the wonderful vegetables and herbs featured in this book and continue to go on new global food adventures in your own backyards.

In addition, I'd like to thank some of the seed companies that helped inspire me to remix my vegetable garden with their diverse assortment of global and unique edibles: Johnny's Selected Seeds, Halifax Seed Company, Annapolis Seeds, Kitazawa Seed Company, Richters Herbs, Baker Creek Heirloom Seed Company, Mapple Farm, Salt Spring Seeds, Heritage Harvest Seed, and Aster Lane Edibles. Special thanks to the folks at Irish Eyes Garden Seeds, who helped us out in a pinch by sending spuds for us to photograph.

photography credits

INDEX

Page numbers in *italic* indicate photos.

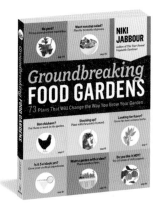
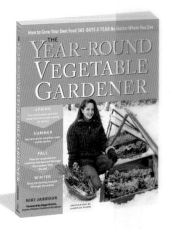